SHAKESPEARE AND MUSIC

Da Capo Press Music Reprint Series

MUSIC EDITOR

BEA FRIEDLAND
Ph.D., City University of New York

SHAKESPEARE
AND MUSIC

BY

CHRISTOPHER WILSON, 1874- 1919

DA CAPO PRESS • NEW YORK • 1977

Library of Congress Cataloging in Publication Data

Wilson, Christopher, 1874-1919.
  Shakespeare and music.

  (Da Capo Press music reprint series)
  Reprint of the 1922 ed. published by The Stage
Office, London.
  1. Shakespeare, William, 1564-1616—Knowledge—
Music. 2. Music and literature. I. Title.
ML80.S5W4 1977   822.3'3 [B]   76-58560
ISBN 0-306-70868-X

This Da Capo Press edition of *Shakespeare and Music* is an unabridged republica-
tion of the first edition published in London in 1922.

Published by Da Capo Press, Inc.
A Subsidiary of Plenum Publishing Corporation
227 West 17th Street, New York, N. Y. 10011

SHAKESPEARE AND MUSIC

[*Frontispiece*

THE LATE CHRISTOPHER WILSON

SHAKESPEARE AND MUSIC

BY

CHRISTOPHER WILSON, *1874-1919*

LONDON

"THE STAGE" OFFICE

16 YORK STREET, COVENT GARDEN, W.C. 2

1922

CONTENTS

CHRISTOPHER WILSON

A MEMOIR

(Reprinted, by kind permission of the Editor, from
The Musical Times of April 1, 1919)

WHEN Christopher Wilson published his master-song,
" Come away, Death," in 1901, *The Times* said of it that it
was " all that such a song should be—fantastic, yet deeply
pathetic, *and as musicianly as a work by a Mendelssohn
scholar ought to be."* The words italicised remain true of
all that this gifted composer left us ; and the pity of it
is that for various reasons, some of which will appear in
the present notice, so little of his work has been printed.

" Chris " Wilson, as he was known to hosts of friends in
Bohemian circles, was born at Melbourne, in Derbyshire,
on October 7, 1874. He came of musical stock on both
sides. Many stories, based on undoubted fact, are current
as to the boy's proficiency on the pianoforte, even before
he reached his teens ; and while at Derby School, where
his headmaster was J. R. Sterndale Bennett, a son of the
composer, he played for the eleven—a somewhat rare combination of talents. There was never a doubt as to young
Christopher's future calling ; and his brilliant career at
the Academy more than fulfilled his early promise. He
carried off no fewer than three bronze and three silver
medals, and was at the end of his third year awarded three
certificates : for the pianoforte, harmony, and sight-sing-
ing. He also gained the Agnes Zimmermann Prize. Wilson
received every encouragement from the Principal, Sir Alexander Mackenzie, while his professors for harmony and

composition, pianoforte, and viola (his second subject) were Mr Frank Davenport (his uncle), Mr Oscar Beringer, and Mr Walenn, respectively. No one was surprised when he capped all his previous successes by carrying off the Mendelssohn Scholarship in 1895. He went abroad—as winners of the British Prix de Rome usually do—and studied under Wüllner at Cologne, von Herzogenberg at Berlin, and Widor at Paris. His gifts were appreciated by his foreign teachers as they had been at home. The beautiful Suite for strings (since, 1901, published by Schott) was performed at Cologne at one of the principal concerts—a compliment that had been paid to only one young Englishman before him, Arthur Sullivan. Moreover, he was selected by Wüllner to "coach" a tenor at the Opera in the part of Tristan—no small distinction. There can be no question that Wilson brought back to England one great asset [1] : he had heard all the great operas over and over again, and it was as a composer and conductor for the theatre that he was destined to make his mark. His sense of the stage and of atmosphere and his love for everything relating to the theatre were remarkably keen ; so his success in this sphere was not surprising. His gifts were quickly recognised by Sir Frank Benson, Mr Oscar Asche, Miss Ellen Terry, Mr and Mrs Fred Terry, Mr Otho Stuart, Mr Waller, and others ; for the two first named he acted as musical director for well over ten years. Apart from the numerous Shakespearian productions for which he wrote the music, his most striking successes were obtained in *Kismet*, *The Pied Piper of Hamelin*, and the Greek plays. In these latter he made no more use of the ancient modes than Mendelssohn had done ; but the result was highly effective and true to atmosphere.

---

[1] Another natural result of his stay in Germany was that his interest in the folk-songs of that country was stimulated ; and he edited for Messrs Boosey the volume of "German Folk-Songs" in their Imperial Edition, the English versions being by his friend Paul England (1909). Wilson's accompaniments and harmonies to these are models of what such things should be ; and a notable feature of the collection is that it contains a large proportion of songs that had never been translated into English.

Opinions are bound to differ as to the comparative merit of the music written for the Shakespeare plays : on the whole, perhaps, *King Lear, Richard II., Antony and Cleopatra, Much Ado about Nothing, The Merchant of Venice,* and *Measure for Measure* mark his highest level of achievement. Wilson was, of course, acquainted with all the traditional music, of which he availed himself whenever he considered it suitable ; the numerous gaps he filled in with unerring taste and skill. Future searchers in the British Museum Catalogue may consider his output relatively small, in spite of the fact that he died in his forty-fifth year. But it should be remembered that incidental music of this kind, apart from the lyrics, mostly remains in MS. None the less, one may rest assured that its spirit and traditions will live on, and that much of it will be handed on by successive conductors for the enjoyment of future generations.

His published works include, besides those mentioned elsewhere in this memoir, settings of " On the Ground," " Take, oh take those lips away " (1906), and a duet, " It was a Lover and his Lass " (1907) ; " Rest in Peace " (words by W. Melville, 1900) ; " If we may not meet " (H. Kendall, 1901) ; " Roses for my Lady " (Harold Begbie, 1903) ; " To a Nosegay " (E. Broad, 1903) ; " There lived a Singer " (Swinburne, 1903) ; " When Roses blush " (E. Lyall Swete, 1904) ; " I bring thee Roses " (F. Stayton, 1908) ; " Ave Maria " for S.A.T.B. (unaccompanied—organ part for rehearsal only—1910) ; three Duets and a Song from *Kismet* (1911) ; and a Novelette in D for the piano, (1903). Of the unpublished works, the most important are the music to a wordless play, " Inconstant Pierrot " (the *scenario* by Sidney Dark) ; a second Suite for strings ; a Mass ; a Pianoforte Quartet ; two String Quartets ; two Violin Sonatas ; and a number of lyrics (including several by Shakespeare and a fine setting of Browning's " Prospice "). He also wrote the music for two pageants.

During the last year of his life, when his health was beginning to fail, Wilson worked much at the British

Museum on a series of papers for *The Stage*, dealing with Shakespeare and the host of composers who have set him to music; here his knowledge and experience, if not unrivalled, were certainly unsurpassed. Of these articles, five had appeared up to the time of his death: (1) and (2), Introductory and " A Midsummer Night's Dream " (October 31 and November 7, 1918); (3) and (4), " Macbeth " (December 5 and December 27, 1918); (5), " Romeo and Juliet " (February 6, 1919). The last of the series was published eleven days before the end came suddenly—for " Chris " died of heart failure in the early morning of February 17. A few hours before he fell asleep he was asked to write the music for the forthcoming production by Miss Doris Keane of this same play of *Romeo and Juliet*— a pathetic coincidence!

Anyone anxious to form some faint idea of " Chris " Wilson's delightful personality, his kindness to all, his utter selflessness, his childlike simplicity of nature, and his humour, should read the two articles on his experiences as a conductor which he contributed to *The Stage* in 1917. But it is the humbler members of his orchestras who probably know more of his goodness of heart than even his most intimate friends; and it is their testimony he would have valued most highly. It should be added that he was a widely-read man, and possessed a sound knowledge of art and of architecture.

A fine tribute to his memory was paid him by his brother Savages—among whom he had spent so many happy hours —on the Saturday night of the week in which he died, when Mr George Baker sang his " Come away, Death " with an effect that will never be forgotten by those who were present.

INTRODUCTORY

WHEN I first contemplated writing these articles it seemed to me to be a very interesting, amusing, and pleasant job indeed. I had seen a great number of Shakespeare's plays, read some of them, and written or conducted music for most. All I had to do, I thought, was to jot down a few notes of what I had heard or read, and out of them make a readable couple of columns. I began to make the notes, and swiftly it dawned upon me what an enormous task I had taken on. I found that nearly every composer, great or small, since Shakespeare's time had been inspired, directly or indirectly, by our poet. True, Handel avoided him (I can find no trace of Shakespeare in the opera *Julius Cæsar*), and I don't suppose Bach ever heard of him; but I feel sure that Beethoven's " Coriolan " Overture owes something to Shakespeare as well as to von Collin, the direct author of the play. But when the plays began to be translated and circulated abroad, composers all over Europe came under his extraordinary influence, and began composing music to his plays or about characters in them.

No music to the plays by contemporary composers has survived. Most people associate him with Purcell, Locke, Robert Johnson, Bannister, or Pelham Humphrey; but all these were born some years after his death, except Johnson, whose settings of " Where the Bee Sucks " and " Full Fathom Five " are supposed to be the original; but, as Johnson was only twelve years old when Shakespeare died, *The Tempest* must have been produced without these songs, or Johnson must have been more than usually precocious. The *Encyclopædia Britannica* definitely says that Johnson's settings are the original.

There are many theories to account for the singular absence of contemporary musical settings of Shakespeare's lyrics : a quite possible one being that he wrote his songs to popular tunes of the day, which everyone knew and no one troubled to write down and print. Many of our great revue composers hammer out the tune first and then get some versifier to write words to it. Anyhow, if one is going to produce Shakespeare's plays and only use settings composed for the original productions, one would have very little music ; and, as he was always calling for music, both in his stage directions and from the mouths of his characters, the performances might please the Stage Society, but certainly would not have pleased the author.

Musically, there are many ways of producing Shakespeare's plays. One is the absolutely " correct " method —that is, to play *The Tempest*, say, with the precocious Johnson's two songs only. Another way, not so " correct," would be to use the precocious one's two songs, and also use contemporary music not written originally for the words, but adapted by the producer. Yet another way is the " broad-minded," and includes any setting of Shakespeare's words written within a hundred years or so. This method is still roughly described as Elizabethan, but if you include yet another hundred years the music is called Shakespearian. After that you get the Old English Wardour Street variety, and, later still, the tambourin school. To some people a liberal tambourin part in two-four time denotes " Old English " music :

(The same figure on the tambourin with the tinkling bells, is called " Eastern.")

A quite good method is to use the best of all the written music and make it into a hotch-potch. This is really a very practical way, and often gives good results. Finally,

one takes the whole music written specially for one play
by one composer of any period, and does it as written,
with no addition or alteration : this is an ideal method
very rarely put into practice.   Even when commissioning
a living composer, managers try to bring in a favourite
number by Arne or Horn, and, unless the composer is a
very strong or a very rich man, his musical scheme will be
broken by some well-known tune not in the least in the
style of the rest of his music.

It is difficult to persuade the average Shakespearian
producer that Shakespeare, Arne, Sir Henry Bishop, and
Horn were not great friends who used to meet daily at
the Mermaid Tavern to discuss incidental music.

CHRISTOPHER WILSON.

SHAKESPEARE AND MUSIC

ANTONY AND CLEOPATRA

THERE is a long list of operas under the names *Cléopâtre* and *Kleopatra* in Clément et Larousse's *Dictionnaire Lyrique*, and in Riemann's *Opernhandbuch*, but it is doubtful if a single one of them can be said to be founded on Shakespeare's *Antony and Cleopatra*. There seems material in it for hundreds of operas, but no one seems to have been inspired to write them.

Sir Henry Bishop has certainly written an " Epicedium," or funeral dirge, for the end of the play, for the production at Covent Garden ; but though no author's name save Shakespeare's appears on the title-page, I can trace no text of Shakespeare's in this " Epicedium." It was produced in November 1813, and Grove's *Dictionary of Music and Musicians* does not mention it. It was sung at the end of the play, and is for chorus, orchestra, solo tenor and baritone. The first and second choruses are laments of the soldiers over Antony's death ; then the solo baritone tells the chorus not to be ashamed of shedding tears, and the chorus sentimentalise over his bravery and generosity. The tenor sings of how he (Antony) was deserted by Mars and Neptune, and tells them to bury the lovers together. The final chorus is quite cheerful. Everyone seems pleased with the monument that has been erected, and " the shout of warriors thunders o'er the tomb." It is not a very dignified production, and I should not have paid much attention to it but for the fact that so little has been written musically on this subject that I thought some of my readers might be interested by this slight and incongruous work.

I

K. H. Graun in 1742 composed an overture to this play which is, I think, the earliest known work on the subject. The only available copy of the score is in Berlin, and, at the time of writing, rather difficult to get at. Graun was born in 1701, at Wahrenbrück, Saxony, and is one of the few celebrated composers who were famous operatic singers before they were composers. His oratorio *The Death of Jesus* takes the same place in Germany as Handel's *Messiah* does here in England.

August Enna, a Danish composer, wrote an opera founded on Shakespeare's play, which was produced at the Royal Opera House, Copenhagen, in 1894; but, with the exception of the overture, none of it has been performed in London. The overture was played under Sir Henry Wood by the Queen's Hall Orchestra on July 6, 1912. The opera was not a success in Copenhagen, in spite of the popularity of the composer and the natural sympathy he would receive from his compatriots. The critics said that he was obviously too much under the double influence of Wagner and Verdi, and, though admiring his prodigious technique in orchestration, gave him otherwise but faint praise. Enna was born May 13, 1860. He was largely self-taught ; but, with the help of Niels Gade, won the Ancker Scholarship, a sort of Danish " Prix de Rome," which enabled him to study in Germany and acquire a considerable technique—a useful possession for a modern grand-opera composer.

Rodolphe Kreutzer, whose violin exercises have driven thousands of amateurs nearly to suicide, composed a " Grand Historic Ballet " on *Antony and Cleopatra*, which was produced in Vienna, but the date is as uncertain as the work's connection with Shakespeare's play. It would seem impossible to anyone who has seen or read the play not to have been influenced by it to a certain extent, and as Kreutzer was born in 1766 he may have seen or read some translation ; but he does not appear to have gathered

the slightest glimmer of the tragedy of Antony and Cleopatra, and he was content to compose a whole series of
numbers, all equally banal, not one of them suggesting
for a single moment either 'of the great lovers or the sur-
roundings. The only redeeming feature of a long and
tedious work is that there is no attempt at Wardour Street
Egyptian music.

Hector Berlioz made his third unsuccessful attempt on
the Prix de Rome with a cantata on this subject. Though
not founded on a scene or scenes from Shakespeare's play,
it was undoubtedly inspired by the poet. Berlioz describes
the action as follows :—" The subject was, Cleopatra after
Actium ; dying in convulsions, she invokes the spirit of
the Pharaohs, demanding, criminal though she be, whether
she dare claim a place beside them in their mighty tombs.
It was a magnificent theme, and I had often pondered over
Juliet's ' But if, when I am laid into the tomb,' which is,
at least in terror of approaching death, analogous to the
appeal of the Egyptian Queen." Berlioz himself says :
" I think it deserved the prize." And I am sure it did ;
but the Grand Prix was not awarded that year, so that the
composer had to wait twelve months before winning the
coveted honour. He afterwards used the music, unchanged,
for that curious but interesting work *Lelio*.

" The Vision of Cleopatra," a " Tragic Poem for Orchestra,
Soli, and Chorus," words by Gerald Cumberland, music by
Havergal Brian, is inscribed to the Southport Triennial
Festival, who gave it its first performance. Though not
an actual setting of a scene or scenes from this play, the
work owes much to Shakespearian inspiration. For instance, though Antony and Cleopatra belong to anyone,
Iris and Charmian, who appear in this work, are essentially
Shakespeare's creations. This " Tragic Poem " is scored
for a very large orchestra, and two choruses, one large, the
other small. In addition to the usual full modern orchestra,
there are two extra *ad lib.* horn parts, making six, and four

trumpet parts. For the sake of " Oriental colour," the percussion list is so unusually heavy that I must quote it : glockenspiel, tympani, bass drum, side drum, triangle, castanets, Indian drum, gong, large cymbals, and small cymbals—rather a healthy lot when they all get going ! The work opens with a slave dance, *allegro con fuoco*, and is marked double *pianissimo*. After a few introductory bars (twelve), the dance proper begins, still very softly and in a curious syncopated rhythm. According to the composer's directions the dance grows " gradually wild and riotous," then comes a slower passage marked " yearning," followed by a long *stringendo* passage leading to the climax, " wild and uneven " ; this presently dies away, and Iris and Charmian have a long duet, the chorus occasionally breaking in, telling how the " Queen is sick for Antony," and how " once more

> Venus and Bacchus meet, and all the world
> Stands still to watch the bliss of living gods."

The music here is very difficult ; the rhythm changes often, every other bar, as does the key ; the intervals are strangely unexpected, and the singer can look for no help from the orchestra. A passage marked " In regal martial style " ushers in the lovers, and we have a long vivid duet. Cleopatra sings a lengthy mystic solo, which is followed by an ominous chorus, at the end of which Antony seems to have died, for Cleopatra sings a very powerful dirge for him :—

> Now all is finished, all is done,
>   My world is dead ;
> And he whose glory shamed the sun
>   Lies shamed instead.
> These lips that frenzied him with love
>   Have death bestowed.

The Finale is marked " Marche Funèbre," and is a short chorus, dirge-like in feeling, rounding up the work effectively. It is a very interesting composition, difficult and most complicated, very restless and disjointed, to most ears singularly unmelodious and unsatisfactory, yet, at the same time, full of novel effects, and to that extent certainly worth study ; but I suspect that none of it ever got on the Southport barrel organs.

Unfortunately, I cannot get hold of **Dr Ethel Smyth's** overture of this name, but Mr J. A. Fuller-Maitland, in his *English Music in the Nineteenth Century*, writes : " Ethel Smyth's genius lies in the direction of strong and even virile work ; her overture ' Antony and Cleopatra,' given at the Crystal Palace and the London Symphony concerts, showed that she understood all the resources of the orchestra, and that she was no amateur." The last six words seem hardly necessary. The composer has since proved her worth in her two operas, *The Wreckers* and *The Boatswain's Mate.*

Schubert's setting of " Come, thou monarch of the vine " is not so successful as his " Who is Sylvia ? " or " Hark, the lark." It is a straight, robust song, mostly in unison. There is a quite unnecessary second verse added by one " N. N." Other but not important settings of these words are by William Linley, 1815, for solo boy and male chorus ; Bishop, 1837, for three male voices ; and Weiss, 1863, for bass solo.

Michael Balling's music for Frank Benson's production of *Antony and Cleopatra* contains, among other very good music, a baritone song to these words, with male chorus. Unfortunately, he did not write an overture or *entr'actes*, but his Cæsar and Antony marches are full of contrasted character, and his " Rose Procession " for the last " Gaudy Night " is really beautiful. Sir Henry Bishop set these words to a S.A.T.B. quartet and full chorus, and by repeating each line several times, and most of the words pretty often, has made quite a long and uninteresting number out of it.

Thomas Chilcot in 1745 published a setting of these

words for a tenor voice. It is a good florid song, with a running accompaniment for strings. The composer omits the fifth line of the lyric for some reason I cannot understand. Surely the poem is very short as it is. In setting it he certainly seems to have found it so, as he repeats several sentences. The line he cuts makes rather a good refrain—" Cup us till the world goes round "—and most composers make their effect here.

Miss Frances Allitsen has composed for Madame Clara Butt a " Scena"; the text chiefly from Shakespeare, the words of the aria by Thomas S. Collier. It is supposed to be the death scene of Cleopatra, and the words are a sad jumble of odd lines taken from here and there. The music is very pretentious, and obviously not written round Cleopatra, but round Madame Butt's exceptional voice. The prayer to Isis and Osiris, with its un-Shakespearian rhymes of " supplication " and " desolation," would sound quite right with small verbal alterations in any Methodist chapel. The aria is vocal and to a certain extent melodious in a " ballad concert " manner, but it is utterly lacking in dignity. A long recitative follows in which nearly every note has an accent on it ; Cleopatra applies the asp to a *tremolo* accompaniment, and finally dies, singing a series of accented high notes, as if the asp were hurting a good deal ; and a few bars of minor chords bring the work to a close.

AS YOU LIKE IT

As You Like It has not been dealt with much by musicians, though one of them, Sir Henry Bishop, has been very hard upon it. The earliest known opera on the subject is by **Francesco Maria Veracini.** It was produced under the title of *Rosalinda* during the composer's visit to London in 1744. Mr W. Barclay Squire, in his article on Shakespearian operas, mentions three operas of this name, by Capelli, Ziani, and J. C. Smith, but adds that they have no connection with Shakespeare's comedy. **Bishop's** pasticcio opera on this subject was produced at the Royal, Covent Garden, in 1819. The overture is a potpourri of so-called Shakespearian songs, simply harmonised and roughly hung together. The first number is a duet for Rosalind and Celia, " Whilst inconstant fortune smiled," words freely adapted from *The Passionate Pilgrim.* There is nothing much to say about it : it seems quite innocuous, but very dull. Rosalind's song, which she sings after having fallen in love with Orlando, is a setting of the 148th Sonnet, minus the two last lines. It is again quite dull. Celia has a long and depressing aria in praise of friendship, the words taken from the 123rd Sonnet. After these numbers it is quite refreshing to come across a cheerful male-voice hunting glee—" Even as the sun " is the title— the words being taken from *Venus and Adonis.* There are the usual horn effects, *fortissimo* chorus effects, and *pianissimo* echoes, all the old tricks, but put together by a good old hand, Bishop. Dr Arne's setting of " Under the greenwood tree " follows for Amiens, and a beautiful setting it is. Touchstone, in this version, is a tenor (somehow I never fancied him as a tenor), and sings a bright little

7

song, " Fair was my love," from *The Passionate Pilgrim*. This is followed by a trio for Rosalind, Celia, and Touchstone, beginning " Crabbed age and youth," the words again taken from *The Passionate Pilgrim* (what a useful poem it is to pasticcio opera composers !). This trio is a very simple one. The first verse consists of alternate phrases by the three singers, who then all sing together, over and over again, the line " For methinks thou stay'st too long." A welcome relief is Dr Arne's broad, flowing setting of " Blow, blow, thou winter wind," by far the best to these words. The next number is a terrible setting by Bishop of the first eight lines of the 7th Sonnet, " Low in the Orient when the gracious light," for male voices. Silvius now has a sentimental song to words taken, slightly altered, from *Venus and Adonis*. The situation is inverted : Silvius sings Venus's words reproaching Adonis, to Phœbe ; but Bishop is undaunted, and " Oh thou obdurate flint, hard as steel " is addressed to a woman ! (By the way, Shakespeare wrote " Art," not " Oh.") Rosalind sings a sentimental ballad to the words from *Venus and Adonis* beginning " If love had lent you twenty thousand tongues," of no great importance. Dr Arne's beautiful setting of " When daisies pied," from *Love's Labour's Lost*, is another welcome relief, and I remember in several modern revivals of this play managers introducing this song when they had a Rosalind able to sing well enough. The next number is a march and dance for the procession of Hymen, and is for orchestra only. It is a good example of absolutely straight writing, with no bother about the romance or mystery of the masque of Hymen—a good workaday march in D major and common time. This is followed by the last number, words actually from *As You Like It*. Hymen, who in the original production was played by a boy, sings " Then is there mirth in heaven," a long, tedious, florid song, full of endless repetitions of single words. It is a curious fact that the beautiful lyric, " It was a lover and his lass," does not occur in this version, though really part of the original play.

It was a great pity that Sir George Alexander did not commission **Edward German** to write the whole of his music for the *As You Like It* revival at the St James's, instead of the Masque only. This Masque is so very good that one would like to have an overture and full *entr'actes*, but one must be thankful for what one has got. The work is in four movements. First, an introduction, very quiet and moderately slow, leading to the " Woodland Dance " in the minor, beginning very quietly, but working up to twelve *ff* bars in the middle, and then dying away. The second number is a very graceful " Children's Dance," *piano* throughout, most ·melodious, and very delicately scored. The last number, " Rustic Dance," is the longest and most important. It begins *allegro con spirito* and *fortissimo*, and keeps it up till the first episode, which is in the same time, but *pianissimo* and in the minor. Soon this is worked up to a big *forte rallentando* effect, which leads into the last theme, *pianissimo* to begin with, getting quicker and quicker and more *crescendo* to the coda, which is *presto fortissimo*. This is by far the most effective of the movements, but the " Children's Dance " is the most beautiful. Mr German's setting of " It was a lover and his lass," one of the best of this lyric, was not composed for this production.

Clarence Lucas's overture to the comedy is one of the few purely orchestral works associated with *As You Like It*. It begins very brightly, the first theme being a rollicking one in Old English style. This is developed until we come to the second subject, which is much slower, and is first played on the clarinet. The whole overture is really in valse time, and the second half of the second theme makes a most interesting syncopated valse. The first half ends with a horn passage, suggesting the banished Duke and his friends hunting. There are no new themes. Those which I have described are taken through their phases in various keys, and the work comes to a sparkling finish by means of a *presto* coda. It is a very lively comedy overture, and not at all difficult to perform.

THE COMEDY OF ERRORS

I MUST just copy the whole of the title-page of **Sir Henry Bishop's** operatic version of *The Comedy of Errors*. Nothing could give any idea of what Shakespeare has been through save an analysis of the music that follows, but I can only touch on that. " The overture, songs, two duets, and glees in Shakespeare's *Comedy of Errors*, performed at the Theatre Royal, Covent Garden ; the words selected entirely from Shakespeare's Plays, Poems, and Sonnets. The music composed and the whole adapted and compressed from the score for the voice and pianoforte by Sir Henry R. Bishop, Composer and Director of the Music to the Theatre Royal, Covent Garden."

I have written this down just as it was printed. I was so overwhelmed by it that I felt sure that neither I nor anyone else could improve upon it. I knew there was only one bit of the play set to music—and not a very beautiful example either—in the ordinary anthologies of Shakespeare's music. It is by Dr Kemp, who died in 1824. He chose these few lines from Act ii., Scene 2, lines 187–191, but Bishop, very wisely, does not touch these lines. He brings in every kind of song and tune, from, as he puts it, " Shakespeare's Plays, Poems, and Sonnets," with no reference to the play for which he was composing music. The overture is of the " potpourri " style. After four bars of slow music the theme of Ophelia's song in *Hamlet*, " How shall I my true love know ? ", is played. A few bars afterwards a theme from *The Tempest*, then a very cheerful subject from *Macbeth*, followed by a bright little thing from *The Winter's Tale*. Then comes an old tune for " When that I was "

(*Twelfth Night*) ; next a melody from *The Tempest* and " St Valentine's Day " lead pleasantly into the catch, " Which is the properest day to drink," from *Twelfth Night*, all preparing the way for " Under the greenwood tree " (*As You Like It*). After this theme is given a fair chance, a subject from *The Winter's Tale* is produced, followed by " Blow, blow," from *As You Like It*. A sad little bit from *Macbeth*, succeeded by a very bright coda from *The Winter's Tale*, brings the overture to a conclusion. But why call it the " Overture to *The Comedy of Errors* " ? There is not a suggestion or a line in this overture, except the one on the title-page, that has anything to do with the play to which that is supposed to be the opening, though it is beautifully printed as " *Comedy of Errors* Overture."

No one minds Bishop writing a potpourri overture and calling it " Shakespeariana," but why call it " The Comedy of Errors " ?— unless he wishes the title to describe the overture, not the overture the play.

The first vocal number in this strange work is a setting of " It was a lover," from *As You Like It*. It is a simple but quite pretty song. The next is a song for Antipholus of Ephesus, words selected from Shakespeare's Sonnets ; it is called " Beauty's valuation," and is a good example of the composer's worst manner. Then comes a strange setting of " Blow, blow," from *As You Like It*. The melody of the first part is by Dr Arne and the refrain by Mr Stephens, the whole arranged for four male voices by Bishop ; it makes a strange medley ! After this one is not surprised to find the " Willow song " from *Othello* sung by Adriana to quite a cheerful tune. Dr Arne's " Under the greenwood tree," arranged for a male quartet by Bishop, follows. The next number is a curious duet for Ceremon and Antipholus of Ephesus to the words beginning " Saint Witnold footed thrice the world," from *King Lear* (Act iii., Scene 4). There is no attempt to bring out the weirdness of these strange words. Bishop then composed a very obvious duet for tenor and baritone, with effective *cantabile* passages and plenty of pauses and shakes. Adriana now sings Bishop's setting of " Come live with me " (Marlowe), quite the prettiest number in the opera, though the words seem a little bold for her, and more suited to the nameless character, the last in Shakespeare's cast. Luciana then sings Sir Henry's " favourite cavatina," " Sweet rose, fair flower," words culled from *The Passionate Pilgrim*, but ascribed by Bishop to the Sonnets. Perhaps this was a " favourite cavatina." The publisher says so, and ought to know, having bought it; but I cannot say I really like it.

The third act is brought to a brilliant finish by Bishop's famous glee from *As You Like It*, " What shall he have who killed the deer? " The fourth act begins cheerfully by Adriana singing the composer's " Take, oh take those lips away," which is really a very bad setting. *The Passionate Pilgrim* is again drawn upon for the next number, a duet for Adriana and Luciana. This is a feeble affair rather in Horn's " I know a bank " manner, and the words are again attributed to " The Sonnets." Sir Henry appears to have no more idea of what a sonnet really is than the London editor who asked a poet for a sonnet " not more than a hundred lines long." A pleasant change is caused by the glee party singing " Come, thou monarch of the vine," from *Antony and Cleopatra*, as an unaccompanied trio. Luciana now sings " The springtime of love," words from *The Two Gentlemen of Verona*, a good florid vocal soprano solo; and the opera finishes with " Lo, here the gentle lark," from *Venus and Adonis*, with flute *obbligato*. This is too well known to need description. I daresay it made as good an end as any other that Bishop could have devised.

I have written at some length on this musical " pasticcio," as this kind of opera is called, because it presents strange points of interest. The persistent way in which no single line from *The Comedy of Errors* was set to music for this production is only equalled by the manner in which Purcell did not set a line of Shakespeare in his *Fairy*

Queen. Whenever modern critics point out the faults in our occasional Shakespearian productions, one can always say, " Remember 1819, the year of the first performance of this atrocity."

It is not surprising to find that Sir Henry Bishop was knighted (in these days he might get the O.B.E.) ; but it is odd that he should have succeeded Dr Crotch in the chair of music at Oxford.

CORIOLANUS

Despite the fact that Clément and Larousse, the French musical operatic historians, give no fewer than seven Italian operas entitled *Coriolanus*, and mention four more, unfortunately not one of them is founded on Shakespeare's play. One great overture that is always associated with the play was not composed directly for Shakespeare's drama but for a work on the same subject by Baron von Collin, a Viennese dramatist. M. H. Laboix *fils*, the celebrated French musical critic, in his essay, " Les traducteurs de Shakespeare en musique," says : " Among symphonic works it is not possible to avoid mentioning Beethoven's ' Coriolan Overture,' and we should have placed it in the front rank if a scruple did not require us to refer only to music directly inspired by Shakespeare." In spite of the character of grandeur and majesty which gives it its stamp, the overture " Coriolanus " was not composed for the English tragedy, and a little story will serve to show this.

A German poet, von Collin, had written a play, *Coriolanus*. To give relief to his tragedy, he took it to the composer of *Fidelio* and prayed him to write an overture. Perhaps Beethoven knew the English *Coriolanus* ; perhaps the stern Roman pleased him so much by reason of his vindictive and indomitable character that one night, so say the historians, sufficed the composer to provide the magnificent pages that serve to preface the work for which we have to thank von Collin. The critics have found, with reason, the striking connection between Shakespeare's play and Beethoven's overture ; but if the anecdote be true, these analogies are a proof of that intimate tie which binds together great men of genius. The overture is too well known to require analysis. Everyone will remember the austere opening, the turbulent principal theme, the perfect melody of the second theme, the wonderful fiery development, and the exquisite *morendo* at the end. Beethoven, one feels, must have known Shakespeare's *Coriolanus*.

Of real incidental music composed for this play very little has survived. Most managers were content to play the Beethoven overture if the orchestra was large enough, and to get through with a couple of marches—one for the Romans and one for the Volscians,—a few fanfares, and a little soft music to illustrate the " home life " of the hero.

Not so Sir Henry Irving, all honour to him. He commissioned **Sir Alexander Mackenzie** to write special music, which it is my privilege to discuss now. The composer has made his incidental music into a suite of four movements. The first number is called " Prelude," and is in C minor and common time. It opens with a vigorous, decisive chromatic theme lasting only for nine bars, and is followed by a very tender and beautiful subject for strings, which is soon developed, in an animated manner, into a *forte* passage, that quickly dies down and enables a tranquil melody for wood wind and harp to be heard. After a little while the trumpets enter with a rapid fanfare figure, which quickly spreads over the rest of the orchestra, and works up finely to the return of the first theme *fortissimo*. All these themes are now finely treated in various ways by the composer, and the movement ends with a brilliant coda in the major. The second number is a march in D major. After a quiet introduction for strings *pizzicato*, the violins give out a martial theme very quietly, and presently the wood wind joins in, and a graceful, rather florid theme for the wood is added ; then comes the first theme again, and the march ends with some *piano* trumpet fanfares. The trio is in the minor and slower ; its theme is broad and flowing, and at its end Sir Alexander introduces a longish piece of complex development music working to the first march theme, which is played for the first time *fortissimo*, but soon gets *piano* again. The coda is quite short and quiet, with a reference to the trio : the music gets slower and slower, and ends *pianissimo*.

The third number is a funeral march. The opening theme is practically the same as the few bars of the prelude, but is developed more lyrically. The middle part, or trio, is even more solemn ; there is a very impressive kettledrum effect, and a fateful subject is played on trombone and cornet in octaves against a strong string passage. The first part is repeated with very little alteration, and the end is fitly funereal. The fourth and last number is by far the most descriptive of the suite ; it is called " Voces Populi," and gives, musically, the effect of an angry crowd being gradually stirred up to great heights of wrath. This is followed by an expressive *affettuoso* theme, mostly for the violins, leading to a new melody, very triumphant and happy, but soon broken in upon by the murmuring of the people, this time sounding even more ominous. After a short appearance of the *affettuoso* theme the movement finishes triumphantly on the third theme in a great blaze of music. No stage music could be more in keeping with the true meaning of the play ; it is all on a very high and important level, and is most worthy of its distinguished composer.

It is of this *Coriolanus* production that a very good story is told. After the final dress rehearsal two stage hands were discovered outside the stage door reading through the day-bill. One said : " Scenery designed by Sir Laurence Alma Tadema ; music composed by Sir Alexander Mackenzie ; produced by Sir Henry Irving—three knights. About all it will —— well run." Unfortunately, owing to no fault of the music, this prophecy was not very far out.

CYMBELINE

DURING my researches in Shakespearian music, operatic or other, I have been often hindered by the strange titles under which works were hidden. Having a smattering of French, German, Latin, and a tiny bit of Italian, I could recognise *The Merchant of Venice* under the title of *Il Mercante di Venezia,* or *Der Kaufman von Venedig,* or *Shylock;* but why *Jessica?* Yet there is an opera founded on that play, called *Jessica,* by a Frenchman named Louis Deffès. *Romeo and Juliet* is easy to discover under the title *I Capuletti ed i Montecchi;* but why *Les Amants de Vérone?* *Much Ado About Nothing* one "spots" at once under the title *Beaucoup de Bruit pour Rien,* or *Béatrice et Bénédict;* but why *Hero* or *Ero?* *The Tempest* is easily discovered as *La Tempesta, Die Geisterinsel, Der Sturm,* or *Miranda,* as is *The Winter's Tale* as *Wintermärchen* or *Conte d'Hiver;* but why did Max Bruch call his opera on the same subject *Hermione?* *Twelfth Night* is easy to find as *Was Ihr Wollt,* not so easy as *Cesario.* Under the fine-sounding title, *Ricardus, Angliæ Rex, ab Henrico Richmondæ comite vita, simul et Regno exitus,* we find an old friend, *Richard III.;* and *Timone Misantropo* almost sounds like a pet name for *Timon of Athens.* The title *Macbetto* is a very thin and seemingly purposeless disguise for *Macbeth;* and *King Lear* is generally called *Cordelia,* operatically. *The Merry Wives of Windsor* is called severally *Le Vieux Coquet, Falstaff, Falstaff, ossia Le tre Burle, Die Lustigen Weiber von Windsor;* and *Antony and Cleopatra* is generally named after the lady. But the greatest surprise I received was when I discovered, lurking under the name of *Dinah*, Shakespeare's *Cymbeline* !

It is an opera in four acts, book by Michel Carré, jun., and Paul Choudens, music by **Edmond Missa.** Carré *fils* is the son of the well-known librettist of *Faust* and *Romeo* fame, and Choudens is connected with Choudens Fils, who publish this opera ; but concerning the composer, Grove and Riemann are silent. The opera was produced at the Comédie Parisienne, on June 27, 1894, and was not a success. There are only five characters, and a chorus of lords and courtesans. The scene is laid in Venice during the Middle Ages. The characters are Mentano (Posthumus), Iachimo, Philario, Dinah (Imogen), and Flora, a courtesan, a high soprano, not occurring in Shakespeare's text. Cymbeline and the rest of Shakespeare's characters are cut. Boiled down, the plot is (I will give Shakespeare's names) :—Posthumus is the lover and beloved of Imogen ; they are not married secretly, as in the play ; Iachimo is so madly in love with Imogen that he forces a quarrel on Posthumus, and they fight. Just as Posthumus is about to fall under the furious attack of Iachimo, Philario enters and separates them. Iachimo then offers to lay his entire fortune that, within twenty-four hours, he will bring to Posthumus the bracelet the latter had given to Imogen, as proof that he is her lover. Posthumus accepts the wager. In the second act Iachimo creeps into Imogen's sleeping chamber and steals the bracelet. At the appointed hour Posthumus realises that, in one fell swoop, he has lost his fortune and his mistress. From this point the action becomes very obscure, involved, and difficult to follow. Somehow or other Imogen and Posthumus realise the truth ; Philario mortally wounds Iachimo in a duel, and the curtain falls on Iachimo apologising handsomely for his shocking behaviour. It will be noted that there is very little Shakespeare in this version, but, really, I have given all there is ; and were it not that the librettists have carefully said, " d'aprés *Cymbeline* de Shakespeare," few people would have noticed it. It is a mystery to me why the authors changed the beautiful name of Imogen into Dinah. I have always associated the name of Dinah with coon songs and the kitten in *Through the Looking-Glass*.

The first act opens in Venice with a canal at the back of the stage. The gondoliers sing a bad Mascagni chorus, and Flora enters singing in imitation Italian style. All Flora's part is written in this manner, and unfortunately the composer has chosen a very bad model to imitate—good Mascagni is good, but bad is——! The music is in a curious jumble of styles: sometimes Italian, sometimes pseudo-modern French, with occasional attempts at Wagnerian imitations—Missa's constant use of intentional consecutive fifths becomes very wearing after a time. The music in the masked-ball scene is pretty, and the duet in which Flora tempts Posthumus is melodious, though the situation is rather comic. Imogen's song at the opening of the second act is the best number in the piece, and it is followed by a really good bit of pantomime music while she is preparing for bed ; but on the entrance of Iachimo all becomes vulgar again. In the last act Iachimo dies to the tune to which Imogen prepared to go to bed ; and if anyone, hearing it, should remember where he heard it before, it might raise a quiet smile. The music is admirably suited to the libretto. Both are in the worst possible taste, and the words " d'après *Cymbeline* de Shakespeare " seem rather in the nature of an outrage. Still, it is the only opera I can find on the subject, and perhaps on the whole I am glad ; a few more *Cymbeline* operas in this style might smash the *entente cordiale*.

With the notable exception of the lyric, " Hark, hark, the lark," beautifully set to music by **Schubert,** very little attention has been paid by important composers to the songs in *Cymbeline*. True, more than a dozen composers, dating from 1750 to the present day, have set those words, and also the exquisite lyric " Fear no more the heat of the sun," but with indifferent success. An interesting story of the composition of " Hark, hark, the lark," by Schubert, is told by the composer's old friend Doppler. " Returning from a Sunday stroll with some friends through the village of Währing, he (Schubert) saw a friend sitting at a table in the beer-garden of one of the taverns. The friend, when they joined him, had a volume of Shakespeare on the table. Schubert seized it and began to read ; but, before he had turned over many pages, pointed to ' Hark, hark, the lark,' and exclaimed, ' Such a lovely melody has come into my head, if I had but some music paper.' Someone drew a few staves on the back of the bill of fare ; and there, amid the hubbub of the beer-garden, that beautiful song, so perfectly fitting the words, so skilful and happy in its accompaniment, came into perfect existence." Two other songs probably followed the same evening : the drinking-song from *Antony and Cleopatra*, marked " Währing, July 26," and *Who is Sylvia?* of the same date—a very good day's work. As for the other settings of these lyrics, **G. A. Macfarren's** part-songs for S.A.T.B. are, as is usual with him, very musicianly but not inspired.

HAMLET

Hamlet offers great scope for composers to show their virtues and their limitations, and a large number have done so from Graun, 1701, to the present day. This is the more curious, as there are fewer references to music in the text or the stage directions than in most of the plays. True, there are many fanfares, Ophelia's mad songs, and the gravedigger's song in the last act ; but, as a whole, music is kept in a very subordinate position. I can find no trace of contemporary incidental music for this play. I should like to hear a real Hamlet tucket. From the text, we know that whenever King Claudius drank a cup of Rhenish a trumpet and a kettle-drum played a flourish, and a cannon was fired to let the Danes know exactly what the King was doing at that time. But, alas ! I can find no trace of a real contemporary Hamlet fanfare. The versions still in use in this country of Ophelia's mad songs and the first gravedigger's song are supposed to be the originals, handed down by aural tradition from mother to daughter, from father to son ; but I know something of the wonderful things, transformations, etc., that appear as the result of aural tradition. I have heard Zulus singing what the ordinary white visitor to Africa is told are native folk-songs ; but these I have been able to trace from their sources, though the original composers, Messrs Moody and Sankey, would have some difficulty in recognising their own inspired tunes ! It is well known, if a story is repeated from one to the other by a number of people, how strangely the last version varies from the original. If this is so in words, how much more so must it be in music, where the varying compass of the voices must be taken into consideration : the singer substituting a high note for a low note that he cannot touch, or *vice versâ*. Still, the songs in *Hamlet* may bear a general likeness to the songs sung in the first production.   I wonder !

Of course, an enormous amount of incidental music has been composed for *Hamlet*. Every producer must have some Ghost music, fanfares, a King's march for the Play scene, and a funeral march for Ophelia. Also scene music helps to pass the time during the frequent scene changes that are necessary in this play, and this has been done and re-done by hundreds of composers, orchestrators, arrangers, and hack workers. But this stuff is mostly ephemeral, and at the end of the run or the tour the music goes to the stores in a basket (the remnants that have been collected from the orchestra), and is heard no more ; unless, indeed, the stage manager thinks that perhaps the *Hamlet* march would suit a situation in the new modern patriotic play just about to be produced, or, with the assistance of a tam-tam, could be converted into a grand Oriental march for the forthcoming production of *Ali Baba*.

On the other hand, several important producers have commissioned celebrated composers to write for them. Thus, Sir Herbert Tree asked Sir George Henschel to do the music for his production, and, what is more, actually allowed it to be played more or less as written. Sir Frank Benson's music was obtained with the scenery and props, prompt books, etc., when he took over the company from Bentley, and is rather a hotch-potch. It has been added to from time to time, but it is beyond improvement. The Otho Stuart–H. B. Irving–Oscar Asche *Hamlet* music was insignificant. **Hamilton Clark's** music to Sir Henry Irving's production I cannot find, even at the British Museum, but I remember it well as thoroughly sound, effective incidental music, a great help to the play, and never obtrusive.

The **Henschel** music was far more complicated. Tree produced *Hamlet* at the Haymarket in January 1892. The

prelude is a solemn *largo* movement, lasting about five
minutes, with nothing very distinctive about it. The
Ghost music is the usual 'cello and bass effect, long *pianissimo* holding notes (octaves), with plenty of pauses. The
cock-crowing imitation on the oboe is most effective. The
triple *piano*, high B flat, triplet dropping an octave, gives
a most realistic effect. The next number is very important.
It is called "Danish March," and I take Sir George
Henschel's word for it that it is one. It is very long, and
serves to bring the King, Queen, and court on and off
whenever necessary. The prelude to Act ii. is called
"Ophelia," and is quite conventionally *affettuoso*.

The fanfares are all good. There is a prelude to Act
iii., *allegro impetuoso*, but it has no label, and might
suit Hamlet or Laertes equally well. The prelude to
Act iv., called "Ophelia's Death," is a funeral march for
muted strings and *timpani*. There is very effective melodrama music while the Queen describes Ophelia's death,
muted strings *pianissimo*, and the clarinets playing broken
snatches of the mad songs. The prelude to Act v. is a
pastorale for full orchestra, and the churchyard music is
for solo organ on stage. At the end of the whole play, at
the cue "And flights of angels sing thee to thy rest," a
female chorus on the stage sings, in three parts, "Good-
night, sweet Prince, good-night," which makes a pretty
ending. I gather this was Sir Herbert Tree's idea.

In addition to the fine "Fantasy Overture," which I
discuss later as a separate piece of orchestral music,
Tschaikowsky composed an overture, *entr'actes*, and full
incidental music for *Hamlet*. It was written for a special
production at Petrograd, and is much the finest music for
the play. The whole is composed for small orchestra,
double wood wind, two horns, two trumpets, trombone,
and drums, and these limitations seem to have suited
Tschaikowsky's genius particularly well. The overture is
founded on the themes of the "Fantasy Overture," but
is considerably shorter. The Ghost music is very awe-

inspiring and original, very *piano*, deep notes on the trombone and trumpets, combined with strange, eccentric scale passages on the clarinets. The fanfares throughout are particularly fine, the first being an elaborate and long flourish in nine-eight rhythm, scored for the full brass, but, curiously enough, without kettledrums; nor are these used in any of the subsequent fanfares. Now, Shakespeare in his text makes Hamlet say (Act i., Scene 4), " The King doth wake to-night, and takes his rouse, Keeps wassail, and the swaggering upspring reels. And, as he drains his draughts of Rhenish down, The kettledrum and trumpet thus bray out The triumph of his pledge." And, later (Act v., Scene 2), the King says, " Give me the cups; And let the kettle to the trumpet speak, The trumpet to the cannoneer without," etc. Now, this seems to me to be a strange omission. It cannot have been done intentionally. Perhaps in the Russian version the text is altered and the kettledrum missed out. Of course, the side-drum is generally used in England, because it is easy to take on the stage, and our managers do not like hiring extra stage kettledrums; but this would scarcely apply to Petrograd or Moscow. No. 3 is a powerful piece of melodrama music, mostly on the Hamlet theme, on the solo bassoon at first, and subsequently taken up by the clarinets, all on their low register: a very sinister number this. No. 4 is another melodrama, very *agitato*, scored for *pizzicato* strings and bassoon, with a very curious and ominous kettledrum figure, frequently repeated. The *entr'acte* between Acts i. and ii. is marked *allegro semplice*; it is a graceful waltz, very characteristic of the composer, and is obviously meant for Ophelia. Then comes a strange fanfare for two oboes, two clarinets, two bassoons, and tamburino: this is long and florid, rather like a street march. No. 6 is a long florid fanfare for two trumpets; the first leading off with the theme, and the second following a bar or so later, in canon style: this is a most interesting fanfare. The *entr'acte* between Acts ii. and iii. is a beautifully melodious movement for strings only, sad, and exquisitely written for the instruments. The melodrama music in this act is the same as in the first act.

Before Act iv. is an *élégie* for strings : one of the most beautiful works of the kind ever written. Tschaikowsky has composed several elegies for this combination of instruments, but none better than this. Nothing more ideal as preparation for the Ophelia scenes could be imagined. Next follow Ophelia's songs. These are all freshly set by the composer in folk-song manner, accompanied very delicately by the orchestra. Before the last act comes the Funeral March, very striking, very *funèbre*, very dignified, and very wistful; in all, a perfect piece of elegiac writing, than which nothing more thoroughly in keeping with the spirit of the play could be imagined. It is on the same lines as Berlioz's " Marche Funèbre" in the same situation. The Gravedigger's song is newly set, to a lively and very Russian-sounding tune, accompanied by full orchestra ; but I doubt the wisdom of having orchestral accompaniment either to Ophelia's songs or to the Gravedigger's single one. A long and florid fanfare for two trumpets accompanies the King's toast to Hamlet (without kettledrums). The Funeral March is repeated at Hamlet's death, and the martial music for Fortinbras is in splendid contrast. It is a short, quick movement, only nineteen bars in length, marked *allegro risoluto*, and makes a great end to the play. The music is absolutely worthy of the play, and is a perfect example of what incidental music should be. Sir Johnston Forbes-Robertson was wise enough to use nearly all this music in his fine production. He did not adopt Tschaikowsky's settings for Ophelia's songs or the Gravedigger's, but used the so-called traditional ones, and I am sure he was right here. But why, after having played the great funeral march as an *entr'acte*, he did not use it again, as directed by the composer, for Hamlet's funeral procession, I can't understand. Instead, he used a march by **Carl Armbruster,** quite good in its way, but very pale after Tschaikowsky. Still, it was a praiseworthy act of Sir Johnston to use the large amount of the

music he did, and he deserves great thanks for only inter-
polating one number.

Unfortunately, the music composed by **Norman O'Neill**
for Martin Harvey's production of *Hamlet* in 1907 is as
yet unpublished.   Mr O'Neill wrote the entire score.
He had already composed an overture built on the
themes on which he draws largely for the incidental
music in this production, and he uses the overture itself
in its entirety as a prelude to the second act, under the
title " Prelude, *Hamlet*."   The prelude for the first act
is sombre, quiet, and brooding, with a very curious cuckoo
effect at the end, which is repeated in the subsequent
Ghost music.   Of course, I do not know the habits of the
Danish cuckoo, but obviously, according to Mr O'Neill,
he is either a very late or a very early bird.   Perhaps he
is cracking an Elizabethan wheeze at the expense of the
Ghost's widow's unholy marriage.   The big processional
march for the entrance of the King and Court is, curiously
enough, not founded on the King's theme, but on Hamlet's
theme from the overture now used as the prelude to the
second act.   The scene-change music before Ophelia's first
scene is founded on " How shall I my true love know ? ",
with varied accompaniment, sometimes simple, sometimes
complex, and once as clarinet solo with harp accompaniment.   At the cue, " Held his wont to walk," there is a
fanfare for the clarinet, but, as in most incidental music,
no kettledrums.   The Ghost music in this act is all founded
on the Hamlet theme.   The prelude to Act ii. is, as I have
said, the overture proper.   It begins with the Hamlet
theme, *allegro maestoso*, very bold and rhythmic, which
suddenly breaks off with a *pianissimo* suggestion of " How
shall I my true love know ? ", which is used as the second
subject, and very much developed.   These themes are
worked out in a complex manner, and there is a curious
fanfare effect before the coda, which is marked *grandioso*,
in the major key, and is very triumphant.   The players
come on to perform their tragedy to a pretty little tune,

quite light and graceful, played on the oboe and clarinet, which has a quaint and interesting effect. Before Act iii. (the arrangement of the scenes is according to Mr Harvey's stage version) is an *entr'acte* entitled " Ophelia," founded on her traditional songs ; but I wish Mr O'Neill would use more of his original melodies. An *entr'acte* entitled " Laertes " is a fine, vigorous number. In the last number of all, on the cue " The rest is silence," we have the Hamlet theme in the major, with sweeping arpeggios for the harp, a gradual crescendo to a *fortissimo grandioso* finish to the act. This makes a fine theatrical curtain.

Karl Heinrich Graun, Court musician to Frederick the Great, composed an overture and incidental music to *Hamlet* ; but as the only known score is in the Court Library at Berlin, it is impossible, at the time of writing, to get hold of it.[1]

Robert Browning's Abt Vogler (**Abbé Georg Joseph Vogler**) composed an overture and incidental music for this play for a production at Mannheim in 1779. Born at Würzburg in 1749, he was educated by the Jesuits at that town, and soon became a famous musician. He was ordained priest at Rome in 1773, but still continued his career as a composer and organ virtuoso. He was a famous teacher also, Weber and Meyerbeer being his best pupils.

Some very good incidental music to this play was written by **Victorin de Joncières** for Alexandre Dumas and Paul Meurice's version. The composer was born in Paris in 1839, and entered the Paris Conservatoire, but left suddenly, as he disagreed with his counterpoint master, Leborne (a very conservative musician), concerning

---

[1] As will be gathered from a similar passage on page 2 and from others that need not be specified, it is clear that Christopher Wilson, had he been spared, would have filled in various gaps before the publication of his papers in permanent book-form.

Richard Wagner, who had just given his first concert in Paris. This work consists of an overture, march, *entr'actes*, and melodramas. It was performed at the Grand, Nantes, on September 21, 1867, the composer conducting the orchestra, and the part of Hamlet being played by Mme. Judith, ex-sociétaire of the Comédie Française. When the play was produced the following year at the Gaieté in Paris, this excellent music was for some strange reason refused by M. Perrier, the producer.

The earliest known opera on *Hamlet* is by **Francesco Gasparini,** and was produced in Venice in 1705 and in London at the Queen's in 1712. The composer was born near Lucca in 1668, and was a pupil of Archangelo Corelli, the celebrated violinist and composer. The libretto is by Apostolo Zeno, and the work is in three acts. The style is very much like Corelli's, florid and melodious. Dr Burney, the musical historian, who wrote a *General History of Music and Musicians from the Earliest Ages to the Present Period*, has a short account of this opera in the fourth volume of his work. He does not seem to like it. He writes (in 1789): "*Hamlet*, in Italian, *Ambleto*; written by Apostolo Zeno, and set for the Venetian Theatre, 1705, by Francesco Gasparini, was brought on our stage under the conduct of Nicolini, who dedicated the poem to the Earl of Portland. There is very little resemblance in the conduct of this drama to Shakespeare's tragedy of the same name, though both seem to have been drawn from the same source, the Danish history of Saxo Grammaticus. But if Zeno is much inferior to our divine Shakespeare, in variety of character, knowledge of the human heart, and genius in its most unlimited acceptation, his drama is exempt from all the absurdities and improprieties which critics, insensible to the effects of music, had leisure to find in former operas." So much for the libretto. For the music, there is an overture, ending in a jig; but whether the curtain rises on the last note of this dance for the " Rampart " scene, is not shown in the score. Dr Burney seems to like the music even less than the libretto. He writes: "There are few songs, however, in this opera which would please modern judges of music either by their melody or harmony." And on the whole I agree with the doctor.

Though *Hamlet* has been treated many times operatically, the only setting that is ever performed is that of **Ambroise Thomas,** in five acts, book by Carré and Barbier, produced in Paris 1860. Boito did the libretto for Faccio's *Hamlet,* produced in Genoa 1865, but I cannot get a copy. Anyway, Boito's libretto would certainly be the best *Hamlet* one ever written. After Gasparini comes a whole list of names of *Hamlet* composers, much too tedious to quote, the only interesting name between him and Faccio being **Domenico Scarlatti,** the famous harpsichord player and composer, whose opera was produced in Rome, 1715.

Thomas's prelude is very short, and obviously connected with the supernatural happenings at Elsinore. The opening chorus is bright, and all in praise of the King and Queen. Everyone seems happy until Hamlet and Ophelia come on, and their first duet opens very sadly. All through this work one gets glimpses of familiar quotations, but there is no close adherence to Shakespeare; rather have MM. Carré and Barbier followed in the paths of Shadwell, Davenant, and Colley Cibber. Laertes, on his entrance, sings a very stirring patriotic song, and manages to get away without any advice from Polonius. The part of Polonius is mercilessly cut down to almost nothing. Fancy a singing Polonius! Scene 2 is a very serviceable Ghost scene, with the clock striking twelve, fanfares and plenty of *tremolo*; and the operatic version gives a very fair idea of the original scene.

Act ii. opens with a short prelude on one of Ophelia's themes, and then there is a long recitative and aria for her (Ophelia). I do not think it would be wise or expedient to give an exact analysis of this work, so I will pass over with but few references.

Act iv. begins with a long and complicated ballet, which is about the changes of weather from which we suffer, and Ophelia's " mad scene " comes in the midst of it. The tyranny of the grand-opera ballet is one of the most cramping things that have ever helped to ruin the fine spontaneity of dramatic art. Everyone knows how Wagner fought against it, and of the final *débâcle* in Paris. Wagner, as a sop to the Jockey Club and Napoleon III., put a ballet in *Tannhäuser*, but it was a logical ballet, and in keeping with the general idea of the opera. But because it was performed in the only possible place in the work where it was suitable, the Parisians hooted the opera off the stage. So why should not Ambroise Thomas have put a ballet in *Hamlet* ? Wagner gave way to his producer, but was firm as to where the ballet should come. The ballet ran on from the overture, and there was no question of a super-imposed ballet. The Paris ballet music, Wagner using the *Tannhäuser* melodies with the *Tristan* technique, is one of the most interesting of all Wagner's struggles against what he loathed so much. In spite of his giving way to the Paris convention, the ballet was a failure, because he would have it in the first act ; but it still serves to remind us English people that we are not the only inartistic nation in the world, though we seldom sing pæans in our own praise.

A very entertaining innovation of our French adapters is that instead of Hamlet telling the players how to act, or in opera how to sing, he calls for wine, and sings a merry drinking song, which probably pleased the performers much more than a free singing lesson or a few tips on elocution. I should very much like to see how Wagner would have treated this scene. I feel sure he would have made Hamlet tell the singing players to use the Italian *bel canto* production, but, at the same time, to sing the words as if they meant something and were not as unimportant as the perpetual A--A—A of the singing exercises.

The usual end of the opera differs a little from Shake-speare's. The Queen, Laertes, and Polonius live, and Hamlet is crowned King of Denmark to music very similar to that which is sung in the first act, in praise of Claudius and his Queen. But there is another ending sometimes played to this opera. It is an ending that ought to make Cibber blush ! Sir Alexander Mackenzie told me he saw this closing scene in Paris. The poor, unimaginative, bourgeois English producer could never rise to such Latin heights. Here it is :—At the end of the play, Ophelia marries Hamlet, and the Ghost, with full melodrama-musical accompaniment, gives them his blessing. It is a dull thing to be a simple Anglo-Saxon !

One of the most interesting things about this opera is that Hamlet is a bass-baritone ; very few people would believe this unless they heard the opera, or saw it in black and white in the score.

A very interesting opera on this subject is **Aristide Hignard's** lyric drama in five acts, book by Pierre de Garal. The composer finished the score in the well-founded hope of a speedy production, neither he nor his friends knowing that Ambroise Thomas's work on the same subject was already accepted and being rehearsed at the Opéra, Paris, which fact upset all his hopes. In this deeply studied work the composer had made an effort to discover a new form, and believed that he had succeeded. The new form con-sisted in this, says M. Hignard in his preface to the score : in the vocal part of his work he interpolates declamation, replacing the recitatives, and fully backed by the orchestra. This procedure, which Massenet employed much later in *Manon*, was undoubtedly new then, and the honour of inventing it falls distinctly to Hignard. The composer was so disappointed at not being first in the field, that even before the production and subsequent success of his colleague's opera he abandoned all hopes of producing his work on the stage in Paris, but published the score, not only to make it known but also to prove that it had

been conceived by him at the same time as his illustrious
confrère's opera.   After twenty years it saw the light in
his native town of Nantes, and its success gave some con-
solation to its composer for his earlier disappointment.
Clément and Larousse, in their account of it, say :
" This *Hamlet* is remarkable in more than name.   In it
one finds much music of a real and high inspiration ;
in the numbers it is necessary to mention, the Platform
scenes are treated very dramatically ;   the beautiful
septuor which follows the Play scene, and particularly the
music that accompanies the funeral of Ophelia, when the
composer finds music of great pathos, are most suitable.
The   *entr'actes*, ballets, and character passages make
delightful episodes, being full of charm and grace, and very
picturesque in colouring.   To sum up, it is the work of an
artist, always learned, and does great honour to the hand
that signed it."   Grove's *Dictionary of Music* does not
mention this composer's name, but Riemann says he was
born in Nantes, May 22, 1822, was a pupil of Halévy at
the Paris Conservatoire, composed much music, including
several comic operas, and died at Vernon in 1898.

Franco Faccio had the inestimable boon of the services
of Boito as librettist for his *Hamlet* opera.   Faccio was born
1840, at Verona, and at the age of fifteen entered the Conservatoire at Milan.   He and Boito fought together in the
Garibaldian Army in 1867–68, after the opera had been
successfully produced at the Teatro Carlo Felice, Genoa,
on May 30, 1865 ; it was revived at the Scala in 1871, but
was a failure.   The work is called *Amleto*, a lyrical tragedy
in four acts.   " Dubita pur che brillino (sortita d'Ophelia) "
is a sort of paraphrase of Hamlet's letter :—

> Doubt thou the stars are fire,
> Doubt that the sun doth move,
> Doubt truth to be a liar,
> But never doubt I love.

It is quite a beautiful song, very melodious and dramatic,
and in a style of its own.   Ophelia is a high soprano.   There

is a fine drinking song for the King and Queen, Hamlet, and
Ophelia, with a chorus of courtiers. After an ironic recitative, mostly addressed to Hamlet, the King leads off singing
very solemnly and slowly the words " Requie ai defunti,"
and immediately afterwards in a most lively style, " e col-
misi d'almo liquor la tazza." Then slowly and solemnly
again, " Oriam per essi," and quickly, " e calice sia vittima
ed altar." The song now continues as a very lively bolero,
until just before the end of the first verse, when the King
sings, solemnly again, " Requie ai defunti," and the chorus
brings the first verse to a close with shouts for the King.
The Queen has the next verse just on the same lines as the
King's verse. Hamlet and Ophelia both have serious asides
in the next verse, but the chorus does not notice them, and
finishes up the number in a fine, reckless operatic way.
The second part of the first act opens in a remote part of
the Castle ramparts. The night is very dark, but the light
in the banqueting-hall can be seen in the distance. The
opening music is intensely dramatic ; the 'cellos are divided
into five parts, and while the orchestra in front are playing
this most tragic music, one can hear occasionally, beautifully
blending with the rest of the score, the lively strains of the
King's private band playing in the great dining-hall.
Dramatically the Ghost enters just as the lively music is
dominating. Hamlet, in an impassioned outburst, calls on
the Ghost for an explanation ; and, beginning very quietly,
the Ghost works himself up to a tremendous pitch of excitement in telling his story. Finally he disappears, and his
voice is heard below the stage singing " Giurate " (" Swear ").
Hamlet, Horatio, and Marcellus finish the act singing,
pianissimo, " De profundis clamavi." This is indeed a
fine concerted number, and much the most dramatic in
any of the *Hamlet* operas. The famous soliloquy, " Essere,
o non essere ! " (" To be, or not to be ! "), is faithfully and
dramatically set, a strange 'cello part giving singular point
to the words " To die, to sleep." Hamlet and Ophelia have
a very elaborate duet in this act, the former pretending to
be mad. The King and Queen also have a duet, entitled

3

" Vieni, compagna," a very pretty, melodious, and light number. The third act opens with the King's prayer ; the orchestra plays a long and solemn introduction, and the prayer is beautiful and dignified. The last number is a trio for Queen, Hamlet, and Ghost. Hamlet upbraids his mother in bolero rhythm, to which she replies tragically, and then the Ghost appears, and the dance rhythm stops suddenly. They sing a grim trio, and the act finishes in a tragic manner.

The next number is called " The Madness of Ophelia." She sings a touching, sad little song, sometimes quite frivolous, but always pathetic, Laertes and the King joining in now and again. This is broken in upon by the populace, who have revolted, and wander about singing songs of pillage and sacking. Ophelia finishes by laughing quite madly, and Hamlet first, and then the King, says " Unfortunate one." Unluckily, this is the last published number, so one has to guess how the opera ends, as there is no copy of the libretto to be found in the British Museum Library. Mr W. Barclay Squire, in his contribution to *Homage to Shakespeare*, says of the work : " It had the advantage of an admirable libretto, in which Shakespeare's tragedy was closely followed." Hence one concludes that the opera ends more or less in the same way as Shakespeare's play.

An interesting opera on this subject is **Alexandre Stadt-feldt's** lyric drama *Hamlet*, book by Jules Guillaume. The composer, a Belgian, was a distinguished pupil of the Brussels Conservatoire, winning the Prix de Rome in 1849. As he was unable to produce his opera in his native country, he had the libretto translated into German, and the work was performed with success at Bonn in 1881, and subsequently at Weimar.

Hamlet, **Franz Liszt's** great symphonic poem, was one of the latest of the series, being composed in 1859. It was first performed at Sondershausen in 1886. The work is planned on a large scale, and is very difficult to perform. So far as I can find out, it is the only Shakespearian work of the composer, but it is a very important one. The main key of the work is B minor, and the greater part of it passionate and *agitato*. The prelude opens slowly, sombrely, and *piano*, with occasional sudden *crescendos* and *sforzatos*, and significant tremolo string passages, marked "stormy" in the score. Then comes the principal theme, a quick, passionate subject, given out by the violins, and presently taken up by the rest of the orchestra. This is quickly followed by a strongly marked theme, allotted to the full strings in unison, and these subjects are developed until the Ophelia music is heard. This, naturally, is very different from the preceding music, being slow, *piano*, with a violin solo accompanied by *piano* wood wind. It is soon broken in upon by the Hamlet music, first on the bassoons, marked "ironical" in the score, and later repeated by the rest of the wood wind. One fresh theme is introduced, also *agitato*, and this thematic material suffices for the composer. After much excitement and working up, we get a return to the slow opening, followed by an *à funèbre* episode, founded on the Hamlet motive, which finishes the whole movement. The end is very tragic, and the whole a notable and interesting addition to our modern Shakespearian music.

Tschaikowsky's Phantasie Overture, *Hamlet*, is dedicated to Edvard Grieg. It is really a great work, full of dignity, strength, and beauty. The twelve o'clock effect is curiously given by twelve *sforzato* semibreves on muted horns, beginning *pianissimo*, and swelling up until the twelfth note is given triple *fortissimo*. The first subject is energetic, obviously for Hamlet, with his mind very much made up; but gradually the theme gets more and more undecided and vacillating, and leads to the second theme, Ophelia, a beautiful and tender subject given out by the oboe. The whole development is long, complicated, and interesting; towards the end a strange quasi-*funèbre* theme is given out on the brass and drums, closely followed by a long passage for full orchestra, marked triple *fortissimo*, culminating in a chord for the wind marked with five *f*'s. Then comes a very solemn and dignified ending, strings muted and everything dying away to a whisper. This work is one of the finest commentaries on the play ever written.

Berlioz's contributions to *Hamlet* music consist of two numbers: a ballad for two female voices, entitled " La mort d'Ophélie," done into English by the Rev. J. Troutbeck under the title " Ophelia "; and a funeral march for the last scene in the play. The words of the ballad are by Berlioz, and are a description of Ophelia's last hours, her wandering by tĥe brook making fantastic wreaths, with many very ingenious references to Shakespeare's scene so beautifully described by the Queen in the play. Naturally, the music is throughout exquisitely sad, and is beautifully descriptive of Ophelia's death. It is not at all difficult to perform, and very melodious ; I cannot understand why Ladies' Choral Societies do not take it up.

The " Marche Funèbre " is not in ordinary march form. There are no trios in it ; it is all the development of one theme. It begins *pianissimo* in A minor, and ends *pianissimo* in the same key. It has a monotonous bass throughout, and Berlioz uses all kinds of drums with his usual weird skill. The impression of many men marching slowly and solemnly must be realised by even the most unimaginative hearer, and it is a work that requires no programme. It tells its own story absolutely to anyone who cares to hear it. There is a tremendous *fortissimo* triumphant effect in the middle, the bass stalking up and down in slow dotted notes, while the rest of the orchestra sustains a slow, heavy melody. After a terrific triple *forte* effect, there is a dead silence ; then a long, deep, sustained note ; then occur about twenty bars of the most hopelessly despairing music I have ever heard, and then the drums again take up their dreadful figure ; and so the whole march winds to a close. It does not end on any note of hope. There is no thought of a glorious resurrection—all is lost, hopeless, despairing. It

would make a splendid *entr'acte* played before the last act
of *Hamlet*, and would put the audience into exactly the
proper state of mind. The march should be oftener used
on occasions of national mourning.

Edward Alexander MacDowell, the best-known American
composer, wrote two symphonic poems for orchestra entitled
Hamlet and *Ophelia*. These works are dedicated jointly
to Henry Irving and Ellen Terry. The composer was born
in New York in 1861, but studied mostly in France and
Germany, afterwards teaching at the Conservatoires of
Darmstadt and Wiesbaden. In these two poems there is
no attempt to tell any story. The *Hamlet* one is naturally
more excited than the *Ophelia* ; but as there seem to be no
Ghost, King, or any of the accustomed secondary characters,
I presume that the composer means exactly what he says,
viz. that the one represents his conception of Hamlet, and
the other that of Ophelia. The result is two excellent, if
rather dull, works. The theme for French horn at the
beginning of the Ophelia poem is the most striking in either
of the pieces, and is the only melody that stands out at all.
It is also very skilfully developed.

Edward German's symphonic poem, *Hamlet*, dedicated
to Hans Richter, the conductor, was first produced at the
Birmingham Festival of 1897. The composer, in a preface
to the printed copy, says: " In this symphonic poem the
composer has endeavoured to depict the character of
Hamlet as stern and relentless, yet in this mood alternately
hesitating and impetuous. The influence of this character
may be said to dominate the entire work. Hamlet's love
for Ophelia is overpowered by his doubts, his distrust of
the Queen, and his determination to avenge the murder
of his father. His fury reaches its height as he stabs the
King. The poison which Hamlet has received from the
weapon of Laertes now begins to take effect, and hence to
the end the music is descriptive of the ebbing away of his
life." This gives the reader a very fair idea of Edward

German's work. It is planned on a large scale for a large orchestra, and is quite the most important serious work that Mr German has given us. It opens with a picture of night, sombre and serious, followed by the inevitable bell tolling twelve. Then a short *agitato* episode leads to a bold theme entitled " Hamlet " in the score. Shortly afterwards come a very pleading Ophelia theme for clarinet and harp, and a fine *pomposo* march theme for the King. All these are freely worked out, and in the middle of this development occurs a very touching episode called "Death of Ophelia." Mr German, following his own programme, works now for his great climax, the killing of Claudius by Hamlet, after which the music grows slower and slower and more and more *piano* till it finally dies away.

It is a beautiful and ambitious work, and well worthy of the colossal theme that it is founded upon. It is a great credit to British musicianship, and I only wish it could be heard oftener.

I have frequently wished that **Grieg** had composed music for *Hamlet*. In several productions I have heard numbers from his *Sigurd Jörsalfar* suite, played as *entr'actes*, and sometimes as incidental music, and they always sounded exactly in keeping with the feeling and atmosphere of the play. I have just discovered the reason. His master and fellow-countryman, Niels Gade, had composed a *Hamlet* overture, and Grieg, unlike some of our modern English composers, who freely set poems and stories immortalised by Handel, was a very modest man, and left his master alone in the field, to our great loss.

Some time ago Sir Frederick Bridge unearthed in the Pepys Library at Cambridge a strange setting of the soliloquy " To be, or not to be," for bass voice, viol de gamba, and lute. Pepys is supposed to have had the music specially composed for him, but, unfortunately, the composer's name is still unknown. " It is a broad, declamatory

setting " (says *The Times*), " something in the manner
adopted by Pelham Humphrey and Blow in their sacred
recitatives; and though it does not differ from a great
deal of contemporary music, it is as much more effective
as it is less pretentious than the strange setting of the
same words in Thomas's version. There is a vague
reference to this in the *Diary* : ' Dined at home very well,
and spent all the afternoon with my wife within doors,
and getting a speech out of *Hamlet*, " To be, or not to
be," without book.' "

KING HENRY IV

THERE have been several operas composed about this King when he was Prince of Wales, but only one of them, **Mercadante's** *Gioventu di Enrico V.*, Milan, 1834, has any connection with Shakespeare's play. Verdi's *Falstaff* opera contains some bits from the *Henry IV.* plays which I am dealing with under *The Merry Wives of Windsor*.

The most important modern work on this subject is "*Falstaff*, symphonic study in C minor, with two interludes in A minor, composed by **Sir Edward Elgar,** Op. 68." The work is dedicated to Landon Ronald, was composed for the Leeds Musical Festival, and was produced there, the composer conducting, on October 2, 1913. Sir Edward, in a foreword, says : " We must dismiss from our minds the Falstaff of *The Merry Wives of Windsor* and turn to the Falstaff of *Henry IV.*, parts one and two." A literary civil servant, Maurice Morgan, wrote a defence of Sir John from the general accusation of cowardice, which has, to some extent, helped the composer's inspiration. This essay was published in 1777, and contains several most interesting passages. In one place, quoted by Elgar, he writes : " . . . a conception, hardly less complex, hardly less wonderful, than that of Hamlet " ; and again : " He is a character made up by Shakespeare entirely of incongruities, a man at once young and old, enterprising and fat, a dupe and a wit, harmless and wicked, meek in principle and resolute by constitution, cowardly in appearance and brave in reality : a knave, a gentleman and a soldier, without either dignity, decency, or honour." This is the complicated character that Sir Edward sets out to portray in music.

Mr Gilbert Webb, who made the analytical notes for the performance at the Albert Hall Sunday Concerts on December 14, 1913, divides the work into four parts:— (1) Falstaff and Prince Henry. (2) Eastcheap, Gadshill, The Boar's Head. (3) Falstaff's March. The Return through Gloucestershire. The New King. The hurried Ride to London. (4) King Henry V.'s Progress. The Repudiation of Falstaff and his Death—and this seems a very wise division. The work opens with a boisterous theme given out on the bass instruments, depicting the mature Falstaff in the height of his fame or infamy, as you will. It would be impossible in my limited space to follow the ramifications of this immensely complicated work. It is a Pageant of Falstaff's life and death. Of the two interludes mentioned in the title, the first is headed in the score, " Dream Interlude." " Jack Falstaff, now Sir John, a boy and page to Thomas Mowbray, Duke of Norfolk." The music here is very quiet, melodious, and graceful. The second interlude represents Justice Shallow's orchard, and is again very calm and reposeful. There is much fine march music for the King's coronation procession, and the meeting between the King and his old companion is graphically and tragically described. The work ends sadly, the various characteristic themes already used being heard again, but in much sadder mode : Mistress Quickly's beautiful account of Sir John's death (in *Henry V.*) is very touchingly musicked, and the work closes on a *pianissimo* chord. It would take a long pamphlet to describe this symphonic poem, and it must be heard and studied often and deeply to be appreciated properly.

HENRY VIII

John Liptrot Hatton, born 1809 at Margate, wrote an overture and incidental music for *Henry VIII.*, dedicated to Mrs Charles Kean, and performed at the Princess's. The overture begins with a slow introduction of a sugary type, followed by a very obvious *allegro*. The themes here are not of much value, and the development does not invest them with any great interest. There is no attempt at character drawing, and the only things standing out in the overture, except its dullness, are a few scale passages for the bells. The first *entr'acte* is called " A Maskedance," interrupted at intervals by Henry's love-song to Anne Boleyn. The dance part has a strange likeness to a number by Edward German, but the trio episodes representing Henry's love-making are quite sad and sentimental. The number ends with the dance music. The next section is headed " Shakespeare's Favourite Tune " (Lightie Love Ladies), and old dances, and opens with a bright country dance called " Wolsey's Wild," followed by another six-eight country dance, " Sellinger's Round," very graceful, with again a dash of Edward German. This is followed by a rather contrapuntal arrangement of the well-known old morris-dance, and the whole movement finishes with " Lightie Love Ladies," said by the publishers and Hatton to be " Shakespeare's favourite tune." It is a broad, simple melody, flowing in style, and, for all I know, may have been Shakespeare's favourite tune ; but I cannot trace it in any Shakespeare reference book. The next *entr'acte* is a prelude and air with variations. The air

and variations, five in number, are made after the fashion
of Mendelssohn's works in the same form, though simple.
There is nothing outstanding about the whole movement.
The third and fourth *entr'actes* are both marches: the
first in the minor, the second in the major key. Both are
good working marches with the regular trios, and call for
no comment.

The setting of " Orpheus with his lute " is interesting.
It is written, for soprano and contralto ; it was first
sung by the Misses Broughton, two celebrated artists.
The composer, in the phrasing of the first two lines,
actually makes sense of them—a very rare thing to
happen to the musician setting these words ; but afterwards
he falls from grace. With only a fair number of repetitions
he gets to the end of the second verse, but then goes back
to the first, and finishes at the end of it, utterly failing to
see how right Fletcher or Shakespeare was in concluding
with the perfect lines, " Killing care and grief of heart,
fall asleep or hearing die."

Sir Henry Irving showed good judgment in commissioning **Edward German** to write the music for his great revival
of *Henry VIII.* The composer took full advantage of
his opportunity, and the music for this play contains certainly the most popular numbers that Mr German has ever
composed. I need hardly say that I mean the famous
" Three Dances," well known and popular throughout
the world. I once heard them in Germany, under the
extraordinary title of " Three German Dances from Saint
Saëns's *Henry VIII.*," but they were these three all
the same — the Morris Dance, the Shepherd's Dance,
and the Torch Dance. They are too familiar to call for
any more attention from me, so I will pass on to the
rest of the music.

The overture is a strong and vigorous work, full of
striking themes and ideas. The first subject is just right
for the King, bluff and overbearing in style, but full of
real strength. The second theme in the relative minor

is very pathetic, and in strong contrast to the first. Then comes a third subject, a very decided march tune, which is used later on in the prelude to Act ii. These themes are all well and skilfully developed, and the whole overture finishes brilliantly with a coda on the "Henry VIII." *motif*, the music getting faster and faster until the end. The prelude to the second act is called "Intermezzo Funèbre," and the opening is exactly in the manner of a funeral march, while the trio has a very graceful subject. This is beautifully broken in upon by the funeral theme, which finally wins a very unequal battle. For the prelude to Act iii. Mr German writes a very pretty, graceful movement, quite in his own style, full of melody and good musicianship. The prelude to Act iv. is a march in the conventional form, brilliantly scored and most effective from an orchestral point of view ; but the ideas do not seem so fresh as those in the remainder of the music, and the whole gives rather a theatrical effect. Still, it is a very good march.

The prelude to Act v. is a "Thanksgiving Hymn" for the birth of Princess, afterwards Queen, Elizabeth, and is good, stirring patriotic English music ; the melodies broad and flowing and the harmonies diatonic—a perfect "Thanksgiving Hymn," in fact. There is a very delightful trio for three of the Queen's ladies (words actually from the play) : "Orpheus with his lute." This trio, which was dedicated to Miss Ellen Terry, who was playing the Queen in this revival, is a beautiful example of the composer's happy knack of fitting music to exquisite words, and adding melody and real vocal part-writing. This number again is very easy to sing, and deserves much greater publicity. On the whole, Edward German's music to *Henry VIII.* is about the most successful modern example of English incidental theatre music. There is, with him, no question of writing down to a theatre audience (generally very unmusical), but a deep knowledge of the play and a very useful knowledge of the stage and how music can help it practically. As performed at the Lyceum, the music was never preponderating, but was always there and always right at the proper moment ; and, of course, the " Three Dances " are rightly immortal.

Sir Arthur Sullivan's " Incidental Music to *Henry VIII.*" in its published form is much slighter, but I have never heard it in its entirety. Much of it is still, unfortunately, in manuscript, but those portions published by Metzler are very interesting. The " Graceful Dance " is still very popular (it seems strange that dances in this piece are always winners), and is frequently played in theatres and restaurants ; and the King's song, " Youth will have dalliance," is one of the composer's best songs. I really ought not to touch on it here, as Shakespeare was not the author of the words, but the song is so much associated with the play that I cannot help myself ; and even though Shakespeare did not write the words, Henry VIII. did, and, anyway, he was in the period. That versatile king, poet, and theologian also wrote music, and very beautiful music, to his own lyrics. The opening music in my edition of the score consists of a long fanfare leading up to a not very dignified march, rather recalling happy old Savoy days than the Shakespeare or Shakespeare-Fletcher drama. The second theme is also rather of the cheap variety, and the third is reminiscent of Rossini ; but I am certain that, judging from the high level of excellence shown in the " Graceful Dance " and " King's Song," much very beautiful music is hidden away in manuscript. Sullivan's setting of " Orpheus with his lute " is one of the most beautiful songs in the English language. It is a very early work of the composer, written long before the rest of his *Henry VIII.* music. The accompaniment is strangely reminiscent of Schubert's *Who is Sylvia ?*

Macfarren's part-song to the same words is also beautiful, and gives the words their real meaning when properly sung and phrased. The lyric is difficult to set, and when set difficult to sing. Most singers give one the idea that

Orpheus made trees with his lute. It is not always the singer's fault, as several composers give this effect. The blame is also a little with Shakespeare or Fletcher for separating the word " trees " so far from the word " bow." Since writing the above, I hear, on the best authority, that of the late Dr F. J. Furnivall, that Fletcher undoubtedly wrote the lyric : so to him is due the blame of misleading simple composers.

JULIUS CÆSAR

Mr Barclay Squire, in his contribution to the *Book of Homage to Shakespeare*, 1916, entitled " Shakespearian Operas," says concerning *Julius Cæsar* : " There are innumerable operas, mostly of the eighteenth century, on Julius Cæsar, as to which Riemann and Clément and Larousse may be consulted ; but it is very doubtful whether any of them are founded on Shakespeare." I myself went through Handel's opera on the subject, but when I discovered that Cleopatra had an important part in the work I put it on one side : I always funk trying to connect a Cæsar and Cleopatra opera with the Shakespeare play. Perhaps Handel was merely anticipating Bernard Shaw's brilliant *Cæsar and Cleopatra*, but, any way, Handel was not dreaming of Shakespeare's work.

A List of Songs and Passages in Shakespeare which have been set to Music, compiled by Greenhill, Harrison, and F. J. Furnivall, does not give one line which has been treated musically.

Of incidental music very little remains ; Schumann's overture I treat of later, and von Bülow's I cannot find in the Museum library or anywhere else ; but **Raymond Rôze's** orchestral suite, *Julius Cæsar*, based on the music he composed for Sir Herbert Tree's revival at His Majesty's on January 22, 1898, is published and easily obtainable.

The overture commences with Cæsar's "March Motive," and here is shown an absolute freedom from Wardour Street Roman music : it is quite as modern as Mr Rôze could be. The next episode appears to be the Conspirators' Music ; it is *agitato*, but of a curious Mendelssohnian simplicity, and leads to a naïve Wagnerian theme, in which the characteristic slow turn is used with great effect. This runs into the Cæsar march theme *pianissimo*, with harp effects, leading up to a brilliant coda on the Cæsar *motif*, with a moving bass and full orchestral effects for the close. The prelude to Act ii. is a very emotional piece of music, sometimes dramatic, often melodramatic, but always exciting and comfortably away from any thought of the historic period. The prelude to Act iii. opens with a fine broad theme for the brass, much of which, curiously enough, might possibly have been played on trumpets of Cæsar's time. After this, Mr Rôze naturally takes a rest from his museum researches, and the rest of the prelude is quite innocent of anything that would remind a Roman centurion, if he came to life now, of his past existence : it is most modern in the 1898 manner, and Professor Ebenezer Prout, had Mr Rôze shown him the score, would probably have told him to " run away and try to be a better boy." Still, there are excellent points in this music, and I wish that more of it were published.

Robert Schumann's *Julius Cæsar* overture, Op. 128, is a fine example of the composer's sonorous and sombre style. Any musician on hearing it could guess the composer's name at first shot, but I defy anyone to guess its title. There is no attempt at ancient Roman effects, the style being much the same as that of his *Manfred* overture, written some years earlier.

It opens in the minor key with a strongly marked theme, rather in the nature of a fanfare ; this is followed by a very beautiful Schumannesque syncopated passage. The second subject, for the horns, is again highly characteristic of the composer ; the whole work finishes very brilliantly in the major.

I cannot see any connection between this work and Shakespeare's play, the overture having quite a happy ending ; but perhaps it represents an early phase in Cæsar's life before he met too many " lean and hungry " men. The whole piece is most effective on the orchestra, in Schumann's own particular way, which I like, but most modern critics heartily dislike. It is very seldom performed, but I should much like to hear it in front of a production of the play.

KING LEAR

VERY few composers have had the temerity to lay hands on *King Lear*. With the notable exception of Berlioz, no composer of the first rank seems to have touched it. At one time Verdi thought very seriously of making it the subject of an opera, and it is much to be regretted that the project was never carried out. With Boito as librettist, what a work Verdi might have turned out in his golden old age!

Berlioz began his *Roi Lear* overture at Nice while he was holding the Grand Prix de Rome, but was stopped by the King of Sardinia's police as a spy. The composer's habit of writing music without a piano did not please them at all ; so he was sent for and interrogated by the chief of the secret police.

" You wander about with a book in your hands ; are you making plans ? "

" Yes, the plan of an overture to *King Lear*."

" Who is this King Lear ? "

" A wretched old English king," etc.

" You cannot possibly compose wandering about the beach with only a pencil and paper and no piano ; so tell me where you wish to go, and your passports shall be made out."

" Then I will go back to Rome, and, by your leave, continue to compose without a piano."

Berlioz finished the overture in May 1831, but it was years before it made any success, and it has never been popular in France.

Some years afterwards Berlioz was invited to conduct a

concert of his works at Löwenberg for the Prince of Hohen-zollern-Hechingen. At the rehearsal the orchestra played the score " with such spirit, smoothness, and precision that I said to myself in amazement, not having heard the piece for ten or twelve years, ' It is tremendous ; can I really have written it ? ' " I am quoting from Berlioz's auto-biography.

The overture begins *andante* with a bold theme for basses, and the whole of the opening is composed in a much more simple manner than one is accustomed to expect from Berlioz. A beautiful cantabile theme soon appears on the oboe, the opening is repeated *fortissimo*, and then comes the real Berlioz. This episode is fiery and *agitato*, leading on to the beautiful Cordelia music. The rest of the work is very long and complicated, but no new melodies are introduced. There are no labels ; each hearer must read his own meaning into it ; but by keeping the idea of Lear in one's mind it is not difficult to get a very shrewd notion of what the composer is driving at.

Konradin Kreutzer composed an opera on this tragedy entitled *Cordelia*. It is in one act, the libretto by P. Wolff. It was first produced at Donaueschingen in 1819. The composer was born at Baden in 1780, and was a pro-lific writer. The only number I can find is the overture, which is an ordinary straightforward composition, that suggests Cordelia just as much as it would Julius Cæsar or Charlie Chaplin ; I cannot understand why such music should ever be written.

In the *Athenæum* of June 8, 1912, occurs the following passage :—

" According to *Le Ménestrel*, a complete libretto of *King Lear* in **Verdi's** handwriting has been discovered among his papers. This confirms the report that he had intended to write an opera on the subject."

Antonio Bazzini, the eminent violinist, composed a fine concert overture to *King Lear*, which was performed twice at the Crystal Palace—in 1877 and 1880. It is really more of a symphonic poem than an overture, but it has no definite programme. Most of the work is very sombre and grim, as befitting its title. I have rarely seen a more restless work from the point of view of *tempo*, and its tonality is constantly changing. It is not in the least the kind of work one would expect from the composer of the popular " Ronde des Lutins " for violin, which is the only piece of his generally known here ; but Bazzini was really a serious-minded composer, and was Professor of Composition in, and subsequently Director of, the famous Conservatoire of Milan. This overture is one of his mature works, and, though the themes are obviously of Italian origin, the development of them shows signs of German influence. The whole work is very interesting and uncommon.

Felix Weingartner, whose symphonic poem *King Lear* is, after Berlioz's overture, the most important work on this subject, was born at Zara (Dalmatia) in 1863, and is one of the most distinguished of living conductors. The score was published in 1897, and performed in England at the London Musical Festival on May 2, 1902. The composer, in his own account of the work, says that it is not to be regarded as depicting the march of events as they occur in the drama (after the manner of programme music), its form being designed rather on the lines of early examples of the overture. The poem opens with a broad *fortissimo* theme, showing the King in his pomp and state. This is followed by a crawling theme, signifying the malignant attitude of many at the Court. These two subjects struggle together, with a third, the love theme, hovering over all. The *motif* of the King in his glory is repeated, but this time the evil influence music gets the better of it. A beautiful theme follows—Cordelia ; but the King does not understand it, and soon Lear curses his daughter in a fine dramatic passage. This section is succeeded by a terrific storm, with thunder and lightning ; the King's theme is played in a wildly contorted form to show that he has become mad. The beautiful Cordelia music now comes to comfort him, and the two are reconciled, but their happiness does not last long. The work ends most tragically. The whole is a very reverent and masterly attempt on the part of a first-rate musician to set down in musical notation the effect of this stupendous tragedy on a finely-balanced brain.

MACBETH

OF the tragedies, *Macbeth*, for some strange reason, is more associated with incidental music than any of the others. "The celebrated music introduced into the tragedy of *Macbeth*, commonly attributed to **Matthew Locke**," as Novello describes it in his edition, is associated in the minds of a great number of people with Shakespeare's play. I have known the work since I was a child. It used to be very popular at village and school breaking-up concerts. I never could understand its village popularity, but I know boys liked some of the strong words in it, and sang them with great gusto. It was sung in nearly all stage productions until about twenty years ago, and is very much missed by local choristers when not performed with the piece on tour. I remember how very disappointed the local chorus-master was to find that Sir Frank Benson was not using it in his later years. The chorus-master thought its absence would spoil the whole play. I have been through the text of Davenant's version, to which Locke wrote the music, and can discover only four consecutive lines and some odd words of Shakespeare's in the whole work. How it persisted through all those years is a great mystery. The music is not even interesting. The four lines immortalised are :—

> Black spirits and white,
> Red spirits and gray,
> Mingle, mingle, mingle, mingle,
> You that mingle may.

For many years this music was falsely attributed to Purcell, but musical historians have finally cleared Purcell of all

connection with it; though long ago he got even with
Locke by writing an elegy on his death. Daniel Purcell,
uncle of Henry, also wrote some *Macbeth* music.

John Eccles wrote music for a revival at Drury Lane in
1696; and **Richard Leveridge**, composer of " The Roast Beef
of Old England " (a song which should be popular if revived
now) and " All in the Downs," also wrote music for the
second act in 1708.

To come to more modern times, **Sullivan's** music is perhaps
the best. Composed for Sir Henry Irving's great production at the Lyceum, it was an instant success. The overture, a very elaborate work, is often done on concert
platforms. The whole of the music is most effective, and
perfectly suited to the play. Subsequently, Sir Henry gave
readings of the play on tour with Ellen Terry, for which
they travelled a full band of sixty performers for Sullivan's
music.

Michael Balling, one time musical director for Sir Frank
Benson, and subsequently for Cosima Wagner at Bayreuth,
where he conducted *The Ring* and *Parsival*, composed some
very clever music for his old chief's production, very modern
in feeling and permeated with Scottish atmosphere: the
Witch music being very grim and mysterious, and in the
cauldron scene very clearly bringing in a suggestion of
Locke's " Mingle, mingle." The Banquet music (strings
only) is bagpipey, and the marches for Macbeth and
Macduff are stirring and in strong contrast, while there is
fine battle music for the close. Unfortunately, he wrote no
overture or *entr'actes*.

Several operas have been founded on this theme, the
most notable being **Verdi's** *Macbetto*, produced on March 17,
1847, at the Pergola, Florence. Unfortunately, Verdi was
not so lucky in his librettist as he was in the cases of

Otello and *Falstaff*, when he had the invaluable assistance
of Arrigo Boito, perhaps the greatest librettist who ever
lived, with the exception of Wagner. Piave's book is not
very inspiring. The opera was never a success. Verdi
could not see Macbeth as a tenor, and bravely made him a
dramatic baritone. The Italian could not understand a
grand opera in which the hero was not a tenor ; and the
only tenor, Macduff, comes on late in the evening. It is a
great pity, as there is much fine music in the work, though
very little of Shakespeare's *Macbeth* gets through. The
very Italian singing and dancing witches seem out of place
on a blasted heath, and the ballet of Scottish retainers
savours of a warmer clime than that of the North of Scotland. Still, the work should be revived.

Hippolyte André Jean Baptiste Chelard was born in Paris
in 1789, and subsequently won the Grand Prix de Rome.
He was one of those Frenchmen, like Berlioz later, whose
music was thought little of in Paris but was much admired
in Munich and London. The adaptation of this play for
the French lyric stage was not suitable, especially at the
Opera House, where the action and words are the most
important things to the public ; and Chelard found that
his harmonies, simple enough to our modern ears, were too
complex for the Parisian audience. He left Paris and went
to Munich, where he revised the whole opera most carefully,
and made a great success of it ; the result being that he
became Court Capellmeister and dedicated the score to the
Bavarian King, his patron. The rest of his life he divided
between failure in Paris and success abroad, again very like
his so much greater compatriot, Hector Berlioz. In this
opera, for the first time, so far as I know, the witches are
given names—Elsie, Nona, and Groem. I think the last a
good name for a witch, but I should not dream of calling
Shakespeare's first or second witch Elsie or Nona. I don't
think Rouget de Lisle, the librettist, better known as the
poet and composer of the " Marseillaise," ought to have
done this. The opera is in three acts, and opens with the

conventional overture of the period—as composed by second-rate musicians, quite harmless ; but one expects something more from a *Macbeth* overture. The Witches have some effective trios, some of them unaccompanied ; and one of their motives was used by Liszt, who knew Chelard at Weimar, and taken from Liszt by Wagner for use in the *Walküre*. It comes quite as a surprise in its original place in this *Macbeth*. *Macbeth's* march is fine and sombre, and the ballet music is quite exciting. One number is marked *tempo d' inglese*, though why a Franco-Scottish dance, produced in Germany, should be in English time I cannot understand. The choruses are broadly written, and the music, though mostly very florid, is often dramatic. There is a tremendously difficult and florid song for mezzo-soprano in the third act for a character called Moina, a friend of Lady Macbeth, and the prelude to this act is a long duet-cadenza for harp and flute. It has nothing to do with the plot, and must have been put in to please two friends who were excellent players or had valuable patrons. The librettist does not stick too closely to Shakespeare's story ; in fact, he gives Duncan a daughter, the Moina just mentioned, and introduces the Sleep-walking scene before Duncan's death. When the opera was performed in London in 1832, Mme. Schroeder-Devrient, for so long Wagner's favourite singer, actress, and companion, sang the part of Lady Macbeth.

An amusing story is told of Chelard's *Macbeth* by Fitz-Gerald, renderer into English verse of the *Rubáiyát of Omar Khayyám*. In one of his letters to the celebrated actress, Fanny Kemble, niece of John Philip of that name, he writes : " You may know there is a French opera of *Macbeth*, by Chelard. This was being played at the Dublin theatre—Viardot, I think, the heroine. However that may be, the curtain drew up for the Sleep-walking scene ; Doctor and Nurse were there, while a long mysterious symphony went on—till a voice from the gallery called out to the leader of the band, Levey—' Whist, Lavy, my dear —tell us now—is it a boy or a girl ? ' "

Surely the world's operatic tragedy is that **Beethoven** never completed his *Macbeth*. He composed sketches for an overture and chorus to libretto by J. von Collin, who also, as we have seen, wrote the play *Coriolan*, which inspired one of Beethoven's greatest overtures.

Wilhelm Taubert's opera *Macbeth* was produced in Berlin in 1857, libretto by F. Eggers. It is in five acts, and begins with an overture in Scoto-German style. The curtain rises on the blasted heath, the three witches, two sopranos and one alto, singing in a very spirited manner. Macbeth enters, and the music closely follows the original plot. The second scene is in Macbeth's castle at Inverness, Lady Macbeth being discovered alone, having received her husband's letter. This is really very dramatic music; and when a servant announces that Duncan is coming that very night, Taubert gives one a fine thrill. Duncan enters and is heartily cheered by Macbeth's retainers, and all exit save Macbeth and his lady, who soon make arrangements for King Duncan's long sleep. The act ends *pianissimo* in a sombre manner. In the second act there is much festal music, a great procession of bards playing harps, and much singing of " Hail, Macbeth, hail ! " Now comes a Scoto-German characteristic dance, towards the end of which Macbeth hears from the murderer that Banquo is dead, but that his son has escaped. The music gets louder and wilder at the end of this dialogue, and the dance finishes with great abandon.

Macbeth summons his guests to the banquet, and Macduff (tenor), with harp, sings a song in praise of Scotland and Macbeth, the chorus joining in heartily. At the end of the song Banquo's ghost appears and spoils Macbeth's party. This act also ends *piano*, Lady Macbeth taking a very remorseful Macbeth to have a nice quiet rest.

The third act takes place in the Witches' cave. Hecate (tenor) and chorus are with the Witches. Macbeth enters and is told about Birnam Wood. The music here is very impressive. The Witches raise up the ghosts of the eight

kings, and they pass Macbeth to a sort of funeral march ;
this also is very striking.   The scene ends with a terrific
hubbub, which gradually dies away, the curtain rising on
Birnam Wood and a male chorus singing " O Scotland, poor
fatherland, how has fate treated you ! "   It is a very
sentimental bit of work, and must often draw tears ; but I
don't think real Scotsmen would be caring about it.   After
this sad opening we are prepared for Macduff's entrance.
He is full of the news of the murder of his wife and children,
and is very vocal about it.   The chorus sympathise, and
the act closes by Malcolm, Fleance, Macduff, and male
chorus vowing vengeance on Macbeth.   The third act begins
with the Sleep-walking scene.   The doctor and lady-in-
waiting are there, and presently Lady Macbeth enters, and,
keeping closely to the original text, the act finishes again
pianissimo.   The scene of the last act is in a chamber near
Dunsinane.   A harper sings a good imitation of a Scottish
song, and then the Wood of Birnam seems to move nearer
and nearer.   Lady Macbeth appears in the last scene of all,
and sings a very dramatic aria, welcoming the advent of
the Birnam Wood, and firmly believing in the immortality
of Macbeth ; but Macduff kills him, and all he says to his
wife is " Farewell, my wife, Eternal sleep is welcome."   The
Witches make a short appearance here, singing " He had the
crown, we have the King," and Malcolm is crowned ; and
the chorus spread themselves, hailing their new King.   By
this time they must have become accustomed to hailing
new kings.   Already they have sung in praise of Duncan
and Macbeth, and now, quite easily, they adapt their vocal
transports to Malcolm, and are very Scoto-Germanic in
their efforts.   Still, the opera has very good points, and
should not die.

The latest opera on this subject is the gigantic lyric
drama in a prologue and three acts, each act having two
scenes, by **Ernest Bloch**, poem by Edmond Fleg, after
Shakespeare.

This work was produced at the Opéra Comique, Paris,

1910, under the direction of Albert Carré. I can find
nothing about the composer in any dictionary of music,
but, judging from the score, he is a modern of moderns.
The work is planned on an heroic scale, and is appallingly
difficult to perform, the time and key changing, sometimes
every bar, during long passages : moreover, the composer
seems very fond of putting in an odd five-four bar un-
expectedly. The opera opens with a prelude, depicting the
blasted heath, and the witches enter one by one. They
are, severally, soprano, mezzo, and contralto. During their
trio distant drums and muted trumpet are heard announc-
ing the near presence of Macbeth, Banquo, and the army.
They gradually get nearer, and finally, with a burst of
grim, significant music, the mortals enter to three horrible
chords and a sinister figure in the bass. At the words,
" Glamis, and thane of Cawdor ! The greatest is behind,"
the orchestra plays a solemn theme curiously reminiscent
of the Valhalla *motif* in Wagner's *Ring*. So ends the prologue ; the orchestra conveys one to Macbeth's castle,
and the curtain rises just as he has finished telling Lady
Macbeth about his interview with the three witches on the
heath. This ingenious device saves the time generally used
in the latter scene, and also saves the audience hearing
Macbeth's account of his meeting with the Witches, which
they have already heard. Further, it allows Macbeth to be
present when the servant announces the advent of King
Duncan, which makes a strong dramatic point, and is
admirably emphasised by the fine Duncan theme ringing
out in the brass. It would take hundreds of pages to
explain in detail this enormous and complicated work, so I
will just touch on a few points of outstanding interest.
Duncan's entrance is finely managed, and his dignified
thanks and praise of Macbeth and his lady are calmly and
peacefully set, in great contrast to all that has gone before.
In the duet (Macbeth and Lady Macbeth) which follows,
the composer emphasises the scorn of the lady for her
undecided husband, and the passage, " I have nourished
children at my breast, and I know it is sweet," has a con-

centrated bitterness in it that is not often found in music. A very elaborate and beautiful orchestral scene-change interlude, founded on the Duncan theme, quiet and very calm, brings us to a court in Macbeth's castle. It is moonlight, and all is still until Macbeth begins the dagger soliloquy, which is set with great force. The Porter's song is very elaborate, and the composer has an explanation, in a footnote to the score, in which he says : " The character of the song of the Porter is this :—The Porter is drunk. He really hears the knocking. He listens, but his troubled brain confuses reality and fiction, and the hammering blows awaken in him the memory of a familiar song. In each verse you get a suggestion of this old song, and only at the last verse he realises that he must open the door." The situation is held with great intensity. The song is long ; there are three verses, each richly varied, and I should think it is one of the most difficult songs to sing ever written. A great *ensemble* number, for principals and chorus, very dramatic and brilliantly written technically, nearly finishes the act ; but by a happy device the crowd rush into the King's chamber, leaving the stage empty save for an old man. The music fades away, the great bell continues to toll, and the ancient sings, very quietly, " I can recall all that has happened for seventy years ; I have seen terrible hours and strange things, but I have never seen a night comparable to this night." (I translate roughly.) Curtain falls slowly.

The second act opens in Macbeth's castle, himself as King. The opening orchestral introduction is very regal, but Macbeth's subsequent soliloquy shows how doubtful he is of himself. A fine series of fanfares brings on Lennox and his followers to the banquet. The music for the appearance of Banquo is most suggestive ; in fact, in suiting the music to the words or situation Bloch is never at fault. The last Witch scene, with the procession of kings, is awe-inspiring, as is Lady Macbeth's sleep-walking scene and Macbeth's " to-morrow and to-morrow " monologue. The tragic feeling never ceases until the very death of Macbeth, when the curtain falls slowly.

This is, I know, a very inadequate description of a most tragic opera, but I have no more space. There are no separate numbers, save the Porter's song, which could be detached from the rest of the work. The opera must be taken as an entity or not at all. There are no attempts at sustained, beautiful melody ; everything is sacrificed to the drama. There are no effective bits from a singer's point of view, and Mr Arthur Godfrey would have some difficulty in writing a really popular selection founded on this work. For a perfect performance, wonderful acting, singing, orchestral playing, and *mise-en-scène* are absolutely essential. It requires months of the most careful rehearsal, but the result would justify all the time and labour spent over it. It should be a great privilege to take the smallest part in a performance of such a stupendous tragedy.

It is the general custom of amateurs to sneer at **Spohr.** True, he was the finest classical violinist of his time, but that cannot account for the general abuse from which he suffers : there must be something else. The something else seems to me to be the curious foresight he had with regard to Richard Wagner's works. When no one, save Liszt, would hear them or of them, dear old-fashioned classical Spohr risked his whole reputation to produce operas by this young art—and practical—revolutionary at his theatre at Cassel. There was something very splendid about him. Among the enormous quantity of music he has written there is one overture, " Macbeth," to which I wish to draw attention ; it is short, it is conventional, but there is a lot of the real feeling of *Macbeth* in it. I don't say for an instant that this is an epic, but it is a very excellent piece of work and quite worthy of the great man, if not great composer, who devised it.

In some editions of **Robert Schumann's** pianoforte works the " Novelette," op. 21, No. 3, is headed with these words from *Macbeth*: " When shall we three meet again ? " They certainly fit in with the first phrase of the movement, and the whole sounds very like a witches' dance, but there is no mention of the words in Peters' edition. I hope it is true, as that gives us another piece of Schumann's Shakespearian music in addition to the *Julius Cæsar* overture and the last Clown's song from *Twelfth Night*.

Raff's "Macbeth" overture is quite one of his most successful works. It opens with a dance of the Witches, mostly for flute and piccolo at first, but getting very wild later ; then there is a sort of dialogue between Macbeth (wood wind and horns) and Witches (their own dance). These themes are developed with considerable skill, and a new one (Lady Macbeth) is added, as are some odd little bits of a sort of Scottish character. There is fine fight-music near the end, and the final triumph of Macduff is celebrated with a very cheerful noise. This overture would make an admirable opening for an elaborate stage performance of *Macbeth*.

Henry Hugo Pierson was an English composer, born at Oxford, 1815, but is still unknown to the majority of his fellow-countrymen. After leaving Cambridge he studied in Germany, where he became very intimate with Mendelssohn. Meyerbeer, Spohr, and Schumann were all his friends and admirers ; and in 1844 he succeeded Sir Henry Bishop as Professor of Music at Edinburgh, but very soon resigned, and settled down in Germany, marrying a German literary lady, Caroline Leonhardt. The inordinate Mendelssohn-worship of his day rendered England a difficult home for a modern English composer : so he changed the spelling of his name from Pearson to Pierson, settled down in his adopted country, and died at Leipsic, January 18, 1873.

His symphonic poem, " Macbeth," op. 51, was once performed at the Crystal Palace concerts, but has been very thoroughly neglected since. It is real modern programme music, and scored for a very large orchestra, including a solo part for the cornet-à-pistons and a military drum. · The symphonic poem opens at Act ii., Scene 2, and is headed

with the words, " Hours dreadful and strange things."
The music is very slow and mysterious, but works up to
a climax on the words of the Witches, " Fair is foul and
foul is fair." Then comes, very *piano*, " The March of
the Scottish Army "—a most characteristic piece, the tune
on the high wood wind, drones on the bassoons, and great
use made of the military drum. This works up to a
tremendous *fortissimo*, and dies away mysteriously before
Banquo's words :—

> What are these,
> So withered and so wild in their attire,
> That look not like th' inhabitants o' th' earth,
> And yet are on't ?

A curious and interesting effect is here made by the tenor
trombone, clarinet, and cornet taking the parts of the
three witches, and playing the themes that fit what the
Witches are supposed to speak. I mean the three " All
hail " speeches. The orchestration is full of sinister
mystery here ; but, on Macbeth's words, " Two truths are
told As happy prologue to the swelling act Of the imperial
theme," the music becomes, for a time, triumphant, though
very wild, and breaks off suddenly for a Lady Macbeth
scene. She is reading Macbeth's letter, and these words
are printed in the score: " This have I thought good
to deliver thee. Lay it to thy heart, and fare thee well."
The subjects here used are the Witches' prophetic theme and
a passionate Lady Macbeth one. All the music in this
section is highly emotional, dramatic, and brilliantly clever.
On Macbeth's words, " If it were done when 'tis done,
then 'twere well It were done quickly," a gruesome little
passage for strings and bassoons heralds the King's feast
music, consisting of curious disjointed wood-wind passages,
till Macbeth's words, " Is this a dagger which I see before
me ? ", when the music seems to drive him to the murder.
After the words, " Hear it not, Duncan ; for it is a knell
That summons thee to Heaven or to Hell," there are two
intensely dramatic bars ; and then, *pianissimo*, is heard the
Witches' prophetic *motif* on the cornet and horn—a fine

bit of musical word-painting. Now comes the longest episode in the work, a magnificent Witches' dance, the composer employing nearly every resource of the modern orchestra. Then, in the distance, is heard the march of the English army, very stirring and martial. At the end of this passage, Macbeth says : " It's ripe for shaking, and the powers above Put on their instruments." Here a great stirring is made in the orchestra, and a cry (violin solo) is heard :—

> *Macbeth :* Wherefore was that cry ?
> *Seyton :* The Queen, my lord, is dead.

Very piteous and poignant music is used in this passage, broken in upon by the strains of battle. At the words, " Blow, wind, come, wrack ! At least we'll die with harness on our back," the music dies down for the familiar dialogue between Macbeth and Macduff concerning the gynæcological manner of the latter's birth, and a few more bars of fight music finish off the former. The sound dies down. The prophetic theme is heard very faintly on the trombone and finally on the horn ; the music gets softer and slower, and so fades away.

I have written at special length about this composer, because it seems so strange that an English musician, a Harrow and Cambridge man, and a pupil of Attwood and Corfe, should have been so much in advance of his time and especially of his country. Born, as we saw, in 1815, he was only six years younger than Mendelssohn, and forty years old when Sir Henry Bishop died. He was four years younger than Liszt, and doubtless got the general idea of the symphonic poem form, or want of form, from the elder master: He was two years younger than Wagner, yet his earlier compositions are far in advance, musically, of Wagner's early work. It seems deplorable that this remarkable English composer should be so utterly ignored by his countrymen.

Richard Strauss's magnificent Symphonic Poem on this theme must take a very high place in the musical com-

5

mentary on *Macbeth*. It is scored for the largest possible orchestra, and every known musical device in orchestration or harmony is to be found in this enormous and complicated score. The poem begins sombrely, but almost at once there breaks in a short fanfare, which occurs repeatedly throughout the work. Immediately after the fanfare the first subject is announced on the brass, and the whole work gets going. Strauss prints a short speech of Lady Macbeth's beginning, " Hie thee hither, that I may pour My spirits in thine ear ; And chastise with the valour of my tongue All that impedes thee from the golden round." In the score the music here is marked " wildly *appassionato*," though *pianissimo* (Strauss here uses the device of *tremolo* strings playing on the bridge with great effect). Afterwards he introduces a long, broad, and very beautiful theme, the sort of theme which his detractors are always challenging him to write, and which he is always writing. Strauss gives no definite programme in his score, and it is up to anyone hearing it to make his own ; but one could not go very far wrong. There is no need to describe the various developments, thematic and harmonic, which take place in the themes before the end of this work. It is long. Ninety pages of closely printed full score take some time to play, and a longer time to describe in detail : so I content myself with saying that anyone can get a fine, convincing picture of the life and death of Macbeth by hearing this work and not bothering whether a certain theme means Duncan, Bloody Child, Bleeding Sergeant, Macbeth, or Lady Macbeth.

MEASURE FOR MEASURE

Wagner's one known contribution to Shakespearian music is his two-act opera, *Das Liebesverbot*, founded on *Measure for Measure*, and not, as so many people think, on *Love's Labour's Lost*. It is his second complete opera, and, for reasons I will explain later, was only once performed; now, seeing that the composer, according to some authorities, apparently destroyed all of it except a couple of numbers, it may never be done again. Wagner planned the libretto during the summer of 1834, while on holiday at Teplitz. He had lately heard Auber's *Masaniello* at Leipsic, and was astonished at the effect of the striking scenes and rapid action of this opera. Could he not improve on Auber's music and produce an opera in which the action should be equally swift? He took *Measure for Measure*, changed the scene from Vienna to Sicily, " where a German governor, aghast at the incomprehensible laziness of its populace, attempts to carry out a puritanical reform and lamentably fails." (The words in quotation marks are taken from Wagner's article on this opera in volume vii. of his prose works, as with the other quotations that follow.)

The score of the opera was finished while the composer was musical director at the town theatre of Magdeburg, during the winter of 1835-36. Wagner had the right to claim a benefit performance, and, having an excellent troupe of singers at his disposal, decided to produce his opera at this benefit. " In spite of a royal subsidy and the intervention of a theatre committee, our worthy director was in a perennial state of bankruptcy," says Wagner, " and before the end of the season the most popular member of

the company, in spite of the unpunctuality of the payment
of their salaries and the offer of better engagements elsewhere." Wagner modestly says: " It was only through
my being a favourite with the whole opera company that
I induced the singers not merely to stay until the end of
March, but also to undertake the study of my opera, most
exhausting in view of the briefness of the time." He only
had ten days for all the various rehearsals. He says:
" Notwithstanding that it had been quite impossible to
drive them into a little conscious settledness of memory, I
finally reckoned on a miracle to be wrought by my own
acquired dexterity as conductor." This does not bear out
the general opinion held in London as to Wagner's conducting. During his season as conductor of the Philharmonic in 1855, he had very severe opposition with which
to contend, especially that of the musical critics Chorley
and Davison (the *Athenæum* and the *Times*) ; but I should
think Wagner was a pretty useful conductor, to judge from
his article about conducting. Wagner kept the company
together at rehearsal by singing all their parts and shouting
the necessary action, forgetting that this could not be done
at the public performance. At the general rehearsal
Wagner's conducting, gesticulation, shouting, and prompt-
ing kept things together, but at the performance, before a
crowded house, there was utter chaos.

Unfortunately, Wagner had allowed the manager, Herr
Bethmann, to have the receipts of the *première* as his
benefit ; and at the second performance, Wagner's benefit,
there were few in the audience, and a free fight, amusingly
described by him, was waged behind the scenes.

It takes Wagner six pages of closely printed prose to give
a *résumé* of the plot, and it would be impossible in my present space to do more than comment on some of the changes.
The Duke, who is the most indefatigable talker in Shakespeare's play, becomes a King, who never even appears.
Angelo becomes a German Governor, who tries to foist
German puritanism on the hot-blooded Sicilians. There is
no moated grange for Mariana, who in Wagner's version is

a fellow-novice of Isabella. Neither King nor Duke ever appearing, Isabella marries Lucio—a strange alteration to make. Isabella, to save her brother Claudio, arranges an appointment with the German Governor at the Carnival (Wagner's idea), and sends Mariana instead. They are discovered, and the Governor expects to be executed for his ill-treatment of Mariana, when news is heard of the King's arrival in harbour. In Wagner's words, " Everyone decides to go in full carnival attire to greet the beloved prince, who surely will be pleased to see how ill the sour puritanism of the Germans becomes the heat of Sicily. The word goes round ! Gay festivals delight him more than all the gloomy edicts. Frederick, with his newly married wife Mariana, has to head the procession ; the novice, Isabella, lost to the cloister for ever, makes the second pair with Lucio." This is Wagner's ending, and anyone who knows the original text can get a fair idea of his alterations.

With the few, but very important, exceptions I have mentioned, he sticks fairly closely to Shakespeare's text. In regard to the troubles concerning the production, much has been amusingly written by Wagner. The police took offence at the title " Forbidden Love." The production was for the last week before Easter, when only serious pieces were performed. Wagner assured the magistrate that it was founded on a serious play by Shakespeare, and, not having read further than the title, the official passed the opera on condition that the title was changed to *The Novice of Palermo.* Wagner says : " In the Magdeburg performance, remarkably enough, I had nothing at all to suffer from the dubious character of my opera text ; the story remained utterly unknown to the audience, on account of its thoroughly vague representation." Of his benefit performance the composer says : " Whether a few seats were filled at the commencement of the overture I can scarcely judge. About a quarter of an hour earlier the only people I could see in the stalls were my landlady and her husband, and, strange to say, a Polish Jew in full costume ! I was hoping for an increase in the audience notwithstanding, when suddenly the most unheard-of scenes took place in the wings. The husband of my prima-donna (Isabella) had fallen upon the second tenor, a very pretty young man, who sang my ' Claudio,' and against whom the offended husband had long nursed a secret grudge. It seems that having convinced himself of the nature of the audience when he accompanied me to the curtain, the lady's husband deemed the longed-for hour arrived for taking vengeance on his wife's admirer without damage to the theatrical enterprise. Claudio was so badly cuffed and beaten by him that the unhappy wretch had to escape to the cloak-room with bleeding face. Isabella was told of it, rushed in despair at her raging husband, and received such blows from him that she fell into convulsions." There was a general free fight, all the company paying off old scores. The principals were unable to proceed with the performance, the manager made the usual speech about unforeseen obstacles, and the performance did not take place. This is the correct account of the exciting second and last performance, told almost in Wagner's own words, of the composer's only Shakespearian opera.

Of the music, Grove says the score is in the possession of the King of Bavaria at Munich. In the British Museum there is a copy of a carnival song and chorus, very bright and spirited, but with no trace of the later Wagner. There is also a " Carnival scene " for pianoforte, founded on motives from the opera, by Geo. Kirchner. Unfortunately, the first half of this fantasia is the song I have just noticed, with elaborate bravura passages for the piano, but the middle episode is much more like the real man. It is a fairly slow, melodious passage, full of interesting modulations, quite foreshadowing what the composer might do. If the rest of the work is up to this form, and if the score is really in Munich, I hope that it will be published, and performed with better luck than at Wagner's " benefit."

As there has been so little music composed for this play, I will give a short account of as many settings as I can find of the solitary lyric contained in it. Probably the first setting of these words was by **Dr John Wilson,** born at Faversham, 1595, who is supposed to have sung Balthazar in *Much Ado About Nothing,* and other similar parts, and to have been mentioned by name in the First Folio edition of Shakespeare's plays.

In this edition (1623) the stage direction runs, " Enter the Prince, Leonato, Claudio, and Jacke Wilson." This particular song is published in Playford's *Select Ayres and Dialogues,* published in 1659 for one, two, or three voices, to the theorbo-lute or bass-viol. The words are beautifully set to a quaint and pathetic air, and there is no verbal repetition. Dr Wilson adds the second verse, " Hide, O hide those hills of snow," by Fletcher, to make the song an ordinary length, without futile repetition.

The next setting is by **John Weldon,** pupil of Henry Purcell, born at Chichester, January 19, 1676, and educated at Eton. This song is interesting, but very florid, and the words are dreadfully ill-treated. Weldon only sets the verse attributed to Shakespeare. The music was on sale at " The Golden Harp and Hoboy " in Catherine Street. Our music-sellers do not call their shops by such pretty names now.

Next on our list comes **Johann Ernst Galliard,** happily named as a composer of theatre music, one of our earliest German " peaceful penetrators." Born at Zelle, Hanover, in 1687, he soon emigrated to England, where he successfully composed operas and much dramatic music, including this pretty little song, which was published in 1730. He was organist at Somerset House, and, I suppose, played the organ while the clerks filled in birth certificates and made out income-tax forms. He died in London in 1749.

Thomas Chilcot, composer of the next version of these words, was organist at Bath Abbey from 1733 until he died (1766). This song was published in 1745, and is a good example of the period, slightly florid, but very melodious, with a charming accompaniment for stringed orchestra. It is a song that would repay careful study on the part of a high tenor. The second Fletcher verse is added in this version.

Of **Christopher Dixon**, the composer of the next setting, no mention is made in Grove's *Dictionary of Music and Musicians*, and all that seems to be known of him is that he was called " of York," and some cantatas and songs of his are in the British Museum Library. This song, published in 1760, has a flowing, rather sad melody, and the second verse is again used.

A glee for male voices to these words was published about 1780. It was composed by either **Tommaso** or **Giuseppe Giordani**, two composer-brothers—probably by the former, who was born at Naples in 1740 and migrated to Dublin in 1761, and wrote a great deal of music to English lyrics. This glee is a charming setting. The part-writing is always graceful, and often very ingenious, the inner parts melodious and interesting, and the whole effective. The composer has adapted this glee for mezzo-soprano solo with harpsichord accompaniment, and a very pretty song it makes.

Jackson of Exeter, as he was generally called, who wrote the celebrated church service known as Jackson in F, has set these words as a duet, with harpsichord accompaniment. The first verse only is taken, but the composer " rings the changes " on the words to such an unhappy extent that it makes quite a long number. Simple, melodious, and graceful, like nearly all of Jackson's secular music, it is not of much value as a serious setting of the words. Strangely enough, it is marked *allegro molto*, and, should this instruction be carried out literally, the effect would be very curious, taking the words into consideration. The composer was born at Exeter in 1730, and this duet was published in 1780. He was a keen landscape painter, and imitated the style of his friend Gainsborough.

W. Tindal, whose setting was published in 1785, is not mentioned in Grove's *Dictionary*, and seems to have composed very little music.   Six vocal pieces, of which this is No. 2, and eight English, Spanish, and Scottish ballads, one of which is a quaint setting of part of Hamlet's love-letter, "But never doubt I love," are all the compositions of his I can find.   This duet is full of clever bits of imitation and good contrapuntal part-writing, and is melodious as well.   Tindal also repeats the words almost *ad nauseam*, and only uses the first verse.

Sir John Andrew Stevenson, Mus.D., composed a glee on these words, which was published in 1795, but is of no great merit.

All that I can discover about **Luffman Atterbury** is that he was a carpenter before he became a musician, was a musician-in-ordinary to George III., sang at the Handel commemoration of 1784, and died in 1796.   He composed one beautiful piece of music, a round in three parts to the first verse of these words, which is really a perfect gem. The melody is simple and beautiful, the counter-melodies are equally taking, and the part-writing is very skilful. What more can one desire ?

THE MERCHANT OF VENICE

VERY few composers seem to have been attracted by *The Merchant of Venice*, though in the last act occurs one of the most beautiful eulogies of music in the world—the lines are too familiar to quote. I can only trace two operas on the subject. The first is *Il Mercante di Venezia*, by **Ciro Pinsuti,** produced at Bologna, November 8, 1873. It is in four acts, and the libretto is by G. T. Cimino, who very freely adapted Shakespeare's story. The work opens with a short overture-prelude of no very great importance, and the curtain rises on a street in Venice with chorus singing and gondolas floating by. Presently Portia appears in a gondola with the Prince of Morocco, playing the lute. She sings a greeting to Venice and its inhabitants, and exits with the Prince, who has not a singing or speaking part in the opera. But Bassanio and Antonio have observed her, and the former has fallen in love with her and tells Antonio about it. They exit, and the chorus, cunningly knowing that Shylock is about to enter, sings a derisive anti-Semitic song. Shylock tells them that he is following a really inoffensive industry, but no one seems to believe him. It would be wearisome to follow the plot too closely here. Shylock has a terrific aria about his daughter's elopement, after which the pound of flesh contract is made; and this scene is really impressive. Then there is a long trio between the three—Shylock, Antonio, and Bassanio—which makes a brilliant finale to the first act.

Act ii. opens at Belmont. Portia is wondering about her father's will, and she sings quite a long and florid song about it. Bassanio enters and declares his love, and a long and impassioned duet follows, at the end of which is a lengthy fanfare, succeeded by the strangest caricature of Mendelssohn's Wedding March I have ever heard. The rhythm is exactly the same, and the melody and harmony are almost identical. This brings on poor Morocco again. The casket business, very much shortened, takes place, and Bassanio, as usual, wins. Then comes the March again, this time quite frankly called " Marcia Nuziale," and the act finishes with the bad news of Antonio and Bassanio's hurried exit to try to save him.

The third act discovers Shylock in a bad temper, still singing about his daughter's elopement. (Really Shakespeare's construction was not quite so bad as his adapters seem to think.) Afterwards a chorus of Jews comes on and sings hymns at Shylock. This seems to make him even more angry. The Trial scene is very much curtailed, and Portia " comes to the 'osses " very much more quickly than Shakespeare lets her.

The fourth and last act opens with a long and elaborate choral ballet, at the end of which (Jessica and Lorenzo being cut out) Portia and company soon finish off the plot ; but, for some probably operatic reason, the full chorus is at Belmont, and, what is stranger, the chorus of Jews break in on it with Yiddish hymns. At the back of the stage a ship is seen on which is Shylock. The Jews and Christians continue singing, but gradually the Christians win, the Jews dying away as the Christians become more vociferous. So the curtain slowly falls. It is a strange and interesting work, and not without some dramatic touches. The themes are mostly cheap and *banal*, and there is little or no dignity about the part of Shylock ; but the work is noteworthy if only for the fact that it is the only opera but one ever written or in any way produced on *The Merchant of Venice*. Also Shylock has one thing in his favour—he is not a tenor.

Louis Deffès, a French composer, born at Toulouse,

July 25, 1819, also composed an opera on this subject, in four acts, calling it *Jessica*. The libretto is by Jules Ardevies. The work was first performed on March 25, 1898, at the composer's birthplace. M. Deffès was a pupil of the Paris Conservatoire, where he studied under Halévy and subsequently won the Prix de Rome. The librettist has taken the elements of his dramatic poem from Shakespeare's play, but has, owing to musical exigencies, very much cut down the work. On the other hand, he introduces a tragic *dénouement* that had no place in Shakespeare's drama. To this book the composer has written most moving and dramatic music, which produced a deep effect on the audience when first performed.

This opera was to have been called *Shylock* and brought out at the Opéra Comique, where the work had been accepted; but circumstances decided otherwise. Among the prominent numbers that stand out in the first act are the song of Antonio, " C'était le soir," and the fine finale. In the second act Jessica has a charming cavatina, and a very interesting duet with Shylock, who also has a fine song in this act. In the third act, at the culminating point of the work, is a delicious chorus of swallows (at the first performance beautifully sung by a chorus of young lady pupils from the Toulouse Conservatoire) ; a poetic dream reverie by Portia ; and a charming ballet ; the act ending with a brilliantly written quintet. In the fourth act are serious songs for Jessica and Shylock, the whole ending with a dramatic version of the Trial scene. The first performance was a veritable triumph for the composer, who, at the age of seventy-nine, an old pupil of the Toulouse Conservatoire, an old Prix de Rome man, and the composer of a dozen works produced in Paris, had returned to his native town to produce the opera and to take over the direction of the school of music at which he had begun his studies.

As regards incidental music, every production of this play must have some. There must be masque music for

Lorenzo and Jessica to elope to; there must be a setting of "Tell me where is fancy bred"; and Portia has her own private orchestra at Belmont. But most of the specially composed music for the *Merchant* remains in manuscript.

Sullivan wrote a very elaborate masque for the Calvert production at Manchester, much of which is published. There is a long and very Viennese valse, full of melody and grace, and a grotesque Dance for Pierrots and Harlequins, with a highly comic cadenza for the bassoon. The Bourrée is the most familiar number, as it is frequently played as an *entr'acte* in the theatre. It is very attractive, but not at all a bourrée on the old accepted lines. There is also a melodious serenata in the rarely used key of E flat minor. These few numbers are all that have been printed.

Engelbert Humperdinck wrote music for Reinhardt's production of this play in Berlin at the Deutsches Theater. This version of the play begins with a barcarolle sung by a tenor behind the act-drop as the curtain goes up. This, oddly enough, is sung in Italian, and the words are not by Shakespeare. Portia is discovered playing the lute in the second scene, cleverly imitated by Humperdinck on the harp. Before the second act is a very stately saraband. For the Prince of Morocco's entrance there is no attempt at Eastern local colour. Obviously the Prince in this version did not bring his own band, and trusted to Portia's private orchestra for his effects, and they did not know his national anthem; so he only gets an ordinary flourish, two trumpets and kettledrums. The same thing happens to Aragon, only the fanfare is different though in the same key. The march is very wild, working up to a great climax, and then dying away to nothing. "Tell me where is fancy bred" is set as a duet for soprano and contralto with female chorus, and makes a beautiful number. After this there is nothing till the last act. The curtain goes up to exquisite music, which lasts till the end of the play.

It is very lightly scored, strings, harps, solo violin, and horns, and every word can be heard through it: so it makes a perfect ending for the whole play. I have never read of this music being performed in England, but I can very strongly recommend it to any future producer of *The Merchant of Venice.*

For Mr Arthur Bourchier's production at the Garrick **Frederick Rosse** composed a great deal of music, some of which is published. It is very good stage music, and admirably suited to the production it was written for. There is a prelude to the first act, ending with a sort of barcarolle; then a melodious intermezzo, entitled "Portia"; an Oriental march for Morocco (evidently the Prince brought his own band for this production); a second prelude, rather sickly sentimental; a good stirring march for the Doge; and a pretty setting of " Tell me where is fancy bred " for contralto, baritone, and harp—very serviceable and useful music all of it. But somehow the play itself does not seem to get the best out of musicians.

Gabriel Fauré, the distinguished French musician, who composed the fine incidental music for Mrs Patrick Campbell's production of *Pelléas et Mélisande,* also wrote incidental music to Edmond Haraucourt's version of *The Merchant of Venice,* called by him *Shylock.* There are not many numbers, but all of them are interesting. The first is a prelude and serenade for light baritone to words of M. Haraucourt's; very graceful and melodious, but unconnected with Shakespeare's plot. The words begin, " Oh les filles, venez les filles aux voix douces." The first *entr'acte,* in march time, opens with trumpets. There is a flowing trio founded on the same subject, and then back to the beginning for the close—a very pleasant little interlude. Now comes a so-called madrigal, not in the English sense of a contrapuntal number in several vocal parts, but a very pretty sentimental song, the words, again by M. Haraucourt, " Celle que j'aime a de beauté," being charm-

ingly set for baritone once more. The " Épithalme " or
" Bridal Song " is for orchestra only ; it is a solemn adagio
movement, almost too sombre for such a comedy as M.
Haraucourt makes of *The Merchant*. The love music is in
nocturne form, and is chiefly a duet for solo violin and
'cello. The last number, headed " Finale," is a brilliant
quasi-scherzo movement in triple time—rather in the
manner of a valse-scherzo. This is the longest and most
elaborate section of the suite, finishing with a well-developed
coda. Altogether Fauré's *Shylock* is an interesting, though
rather slight, addition to our very scanty amount of music
for this play.

THE MERRY WIVES OF WINDSOR

It is a curious thing that, though critics are unanimous in saying that *The Merry Wives of Windsor* is the weakest comedy Shakespeare ever wrote, it has directly inspired one opera of first-class importance—Verdi's *Falstaff*, by some considered the finest comic opera in the world ; also Nicolai's *Merry Wives of Windsor*, a first-rate opera in the second division, as it were, still constantly played in Germany, and here by the Carl Rosa Opera Company ; and Balfe's comic opera *Falstaff*, produced at Her Majesty's, July 19, 1838. This work is not so easy to place ; it is essentially Italian music, and shows how wonderfully adaptable Balfe's genius was.

Braham, Parry, and **Horn** wrote numbers for a musical version of this play, which was produced in London in 1823, but I cannot trace the score nor any of the numbers.

We will take **Balfe's** opera first. There was a fine cast for the first production—Grisi, Rubini, Tamburini, with Lablache as Falstaff : so the work had every opportunity, as far as singers were concerned, but it never passed into the opera repertory, and few people now have heard of it. Perhaps the libretto by S. M. Maggioni may have helped *Falstaff* into its present oblivion. The work opens with a conventional overture, a slow introduction and a quick second part, getting quicker towards the end—the sort of overture that would suit almost any comedy-opera as well as *The Merry Wives*. After the overture comes a duet for Page and Ford ; then Falstaff's entrance and song.

It is impossible to follow the plot clearly, as there is a great deal of spoken dialogue; but all the principals have very "fat" bits. The composer was obviously writing for singers whom he knew well, and he did not bother much about character, colour, Windsor, or Queen Elizabeth's time; everything is perfectly vocal, and the melodies are quite pleasant.

Balfe certainly had a wonderful gift for melody, but there is no drama at all in the work. Parts of it would sound quite well in a concert-hall, but I could not trust it on the stage. At the end, instead of fairies tormenting Sir John, a chorus of witches is introduced for that purpose, and they do it quite effectively. The work ends with a brilliant *ensemble* for the principals and chorus, with Grisi "coloraturing" all over the place. The opera is only in two acts, so a good deal of plot is omitted; still, the work is interesting, if merely from the fact that Balfe is the only British composer who has written an opera, *The Bohemian Girl*, which has been played, and is being played, all over the world. It is the fashion for "superior people" to sneer at Balfe, but *The Bohemian Girl* is the sole English opera in the international repertory.

Nicolai's opera, *Die lustigen Weiber von Windsor*, book by Mosenthal, produced at Berlin in 1849, is now a classic. The overture is quite beautiful; the second subject so attracted Wagner that he "pinched" it and put it into the *Meistersinger*. The libretto is very well done, too. Although none of the rest of the opera quite reaches this high level, all is very good.

After the overture, Mistress Page and Mistress Ford enter with their letters, and the plot gets under way at once. No tiresome preliminary chorus, but straight to the story. In this charming duet is hatched the plot for the undoing of Falstaff. Fenton is made into a much larger and more important *rôle* than Shakespeare conceived; in point of fact, he is the solo tenor lover, and much very pretty music is given to him. All Sir John's music is very expressive

6

of the man, and, though vocal, is suited to the character. With the exception of the enlargement of Master Fenton's part, Nicolai's librettist sticks closely to Shakespeare's text; but there are occasional excrescences, mostly harmless. At the opening of the second act, Falstaff sings a song, with male chorus, the words of which begin with the famous Clown's song at the end of *Twelfth Night*, "When that I was and a little tiny boy"; but after a few lines it grows into a drinking song. Anyway, there's some Shakespeare in it, and it is a first-rate number.

The third act opens with a ballad about Herne the Hunter and his oak for Mistress "Reich" (Ford). It is a very weird and effective song, and in excellent contrast to the music which has preceded it. Sweet Anne Page also has much more to do in this version of the story than in Shakespeare's; but in opera one must have young lovers, and Falstaff and Mistresses Ford and Page are not quite romantic enough for the average opera audience. The grotesque music for Slender and Dr Caius is wonderfully done, and full of quiet humour. After the "Herne" ballad Sweet Anne Page sings a long and almost tiresome aria, but this is followed by the Moon chorus scene, which opens with the same *motif* as the overture. The orchestra plays the beautiful melody, and the chorus sustains long, *pianissimo* six-part harmonies. The whole effect is very fine. Next comes a ballet with chorus of fairies, also on themes used in the overture. Whenever Nicolai employs a theme from the overture the whole work seems to rise in value and become quite first-rate. With Fenton disguised as Oberon, King of the Fairies, and Anne Page as Titania, Falstaff is "put through the hoops," even as he is in Shakespeare's play, and a very melodious trio begins the finale. This is sung by the three ladies—Anne, Mistress Page, and Mistress Ford. Near the end Falstaff joins in, and for the last fourteen bars principals and chorus sing an *ensemble*.

It is indeed a very merry work, and curiously Shakespearian; all the parts are showy to sing and to act, the music, though full of character, is thoroughly vocal, and the orchestration is never too heavy for the singers. As a comic opera it is quite one of the best in the world, and fully deserves its place in the repertory of opera for all time.

We now come to the third opera founded on *The Merry Wives of Windsor*, **Verdi's** *Falstaff*, libretto by Boito. After the production of *Otello*, 1887, the composer was silent operatically; but in 1893, at the age of eighty, he produced *Falstaff*, and astounded the entire musical world. The work was produced at the Scala, Milan, February 9, and its success was instantaneous. The book by Boito is, as the score says, " derived from Shakespeare's *Merry Wives of Windsor*, and from certain passages of *Henry IV*. having relation to the personality of Falstaff," and is a masterpiece of construction and adaptation.

The opera is in three acts, each act being in two parts. Shallow, Page, Slender, Sir Hugh, Nym, Simple, and Rugby all go. Certain lines have to be transposed. For instance, in Act i., Scene 1, Caius speaks Shallow's lines, beginning " You have beaten my men "; but these things are necessary in converting a five-act comedy, with two scenes, into a three-act lyrical comedy with six scenes. Sweet Anne Page becomes Annetta Ford, and her part and Master Fenton's are much written up; in fact, they become a very pretty pair of lovers, and their frequent love-duets are beautifully melodious, and never sentimental. Bardolph (tenor) becomes an important part, and he pursues his old master after his dismissal with the utmost malignancy. The scene is Windsor in the time of Henry IV. Falstaff is a baritone. Victor Maurel, the great French baritone, created the part.

As is usual with this composer's later work, there is no overture, the curtain rising on the interior of the Garter Inn at the fourth bar of an *allegro vivace*. Sir John has just sealed the two love-letters. Dr Caius (tenor) enters angrily and abuses Falstaff nearly in Shallow's words; Falstaff pays no attention, but calls for sherry, and in a brilliant scene the Doctor accuses Falstaff and his followers of making him drunk and robbing him. After Caius's exit, Sir John calls for his bill and sings a song of his wandering from inn to inn, following the light shed by Bardolph's nose, and setting forth how much it has cost him (Falstaff) to get it into its present condition. He then produces the letters, and Pistol and Bardolph refuse to bear them. Falstaff bundles them out of the room and the scene ends. The whole of the music in these comedy scenes is as light as air, the action is wonderfully swift, and every *nuance* in the words is reflected in the orchestration. It is only necessary to comment on a few features, as the original story is so well known and Boito follows it fairly closely now. There are no real numbers that can be separated from the main body ; no songs or concerted pieces that it would be wise to perform apart from the context : the whole work is so welded into one homogeneous whole that it would be sacrilege to do scraps on the concert platform. There are no numbers, like the " Preis " song or Hans Sachs' soliloquies from Wagner's great comic opera, that can be performed with great effect at concerts : with Verdi's *Falstaff* it is all or nothing. The reading of the letter by Mistress Ford makes a fine comic effect, and the unaccompanied quartet for the four ladies—Page, Ford, Sweet Anne, and Mrs Quickly—that follows it is a rare bit of vocal writing. The concerted writing throughout is splendid— the counterpoint is *never* obtrusive, but always there,—and the orchestration a wonderful combination of lightness and strength.

To return to the plot. Falstaff comes only once to Ford's house, and is thrown out of a window into the Thames, so never escapes as the wise woman of Brentford. A very amusing effect, though not in Shakespeare, is obtained during Ford's mad search for Sir John. Fenton and Anne Page have hidden behind a curtain. In the middle of the fearful din everyone is making there comes a sudden pause, during which the lovers kiss audibly. Ford at once thinks it is Sir John and his wife, creeps up to the arras, jerks it aside, and discloses his daughter and her forbidden lover, much to Ford's anger and the lovers' mutual embarrassment! During this act Falstaff sings to Mistress Ford the fine song about his youth, " Once I was page to the Duke of Norfolk."

Though Verdi does not use the *leit-motif* in the ordinary sense of the word, much use is made of a triplet figure. Mistress Quickly employs it first to announce to Sir John his appointment with Mistress Ford. It is used by Sir John when he announces to Ford, disguised as Brook, his appointment with Ford's wife. Unfortunately, the original Italian cannot be, or has not been, rendered into the same number of syllables in the English version (I am speaking of Ricordi's edition), so there is one syllable missing, which spoils the whole effect. This figure is used wonderfully as an accompaniment during the duet that follows, and the eighty-year-old composer gets heaps of natural boyish fun (though technically marvellous) out of those six notes.

The first part of the third act opens with, for Verdi, quite a long introduction, *agitato* in nature, on the theme that interrupts Falstaff's love-making in the previous act. The scene is the exterior of the Garter Inn. Falstaff is alone, and sings his famous soliloquy on the wicked, treacherous world. He calls for wine, drinks deeply, and begins to feel better. He mixes the sack with the Thames water he has swallowed, and sings, " How sweet it is to drink good wine while basking in the sunshine." Mistress Quickly comes on, and makes the appointment for Herne's oak at midnight. She begins the story of Herne the Hunter very impressively, and Mistress Page finishes it.

The next and last scene takes place a little before midnight, at the oak in Windsor Park. Anne Page and Fenton open with a love-duet, and as the bell strikes twelve Sir John enters wearing a pair of antlers. After a short scene with Mistress Page, Anne Page is heard as Fairy Queen summoning her wood nymphs, dryads, and goblins. Falstaff falls on his face, and the fairies enter. There is a long and beautiful sort of choral ballet, in which Falstaff is badly treated by everyone, especially by Bardolph. In

the hubbub Dr Caius elopes with Bardolph disguised as
Anne Page, and Fenton and Anne manage to get Ford's
consent to their marriage.   Then comes the great moment
of all.   All parties are reconciled ; Ford invites everyone
to carouse at his house, and Sir John Falstaff leads off
with the subject of the great choral fugue that forms the
finale.   The words begin, " Jesting is man's vocation," etc.
Fenton takes the answer, then Dame Quickly, then Mistress
Ford.   At first the orchestration is very light, but as the
rest join in it grows heavier.   Mistress Page then enters
with the subject, followed by Sweet Anne in *stretto*,
Pistol meanwhile starting with the counter-subject, closely
followed by Ford, with Dr Caius in *stretto*.   It would take
too long to describe the ramifications of this, as Browning
says of another, " mountainous fugue," but it is one of the
most superb pieces of vocal fugal writing extant, and makes
one of the finest endings to an opera the brain of man
has ever conceived.

The idea of having a great fugue in eight and ten parts,
with a full chorus and orchestra, quite independent of the
solo parts, to finish a comic opera was a stroke of genius
that could only have occurred to a supreme mind, and
could only have been carried out by one of the great
musical and dramatic geniuses of the world.   It is extra-
ordinarily successful, and its daring is gloriously vindicated.
Let those lovers of musical comedy, ragtime, and sentimental ballads who sneer at fugue, counterpoint, form, and
technique hear this, and wonder.   It does not sound very
complicated or difficult, but really it is quite as complex
as the finale of Mozart's " Jupiter " Symphony, the " Cum
Sancto Spiritu " from Bach's B minor Mass, or the great
fugato finale from the third act of Wagner's *Meistersinger*.
Verdi and Mozart make the numbers I have spoken of
sound simple and almost easy ; Bach and Wagner sound
as difficult as they are, and all are equally difficult at
bedrock.

I have written a great deal on this work, though no
number of pages of mine could do any kind of justice to

it ; but if I have helped one reader to a little fuller under-
standing of this great comic opera I shall have " acquired
grace," and, anyhow, that is something.

In 1856, at the Lyric, Paris, **Adolphe Adam** produced his
one-act comic opera *Falstaffe*, with a libretto by MM. Saint
Georges and Leunen.   He was born in Paris in 1803, and
was a pupil of Boieldieu at the Conservatoire.   The music
is very light and fairly melodious, but quite unambitious,
and has been described by a French musical critic, very
justly, as mediocre.   There is a valse in it which was
popular for a time, and a few catchy numbers, but the
critic was right—mediocre is the word.

There is a song by **J. L. Hatton** entitled " Falstaff's
Song : Give me a cup of sack, boy."   But I cannot find
the words in my edition of Shakespeare's plays and poems.
It begins :

> A full, flowing cup of old sack give me, boy ;
> For sack clears the head, clears the heart.

I don't think the words are Shakespeare's, in spite of
the printed title-page before me.   The music is in the
composer's well-known " Simon the Cellarer " style ; only,
unfortunately, the tune is not so good.   The words get
sillier as the song continues, so that if I had been the
boy I should have given the singer prussic acid instead
of the sack he so repeatedly calls for.

A MIDSUMMER NIGHT'S DREAM

FROM a musical point of view one of the most important of Shakespeare's plays is *A Midsummer Night's Dream*. It is possible to use nothing but Mendelssohn's music for this play, but I have never heard it in England without additional numbers. Sir Frank Benson, in his poetical production, used all the original music, but also included a song by Cooke, "Over hill, over dale," for the first singing fairy, and a duet, "I know a bank," by Horn, for first and second singing fairies: the latter a very boring work and quite out of keeping with the rest of the music. There is no reason why these words should be sung at all: they should be spoken by Oberon. Sir Herbert Tree had them sung to the tune of "Auf Flügeln des Gesanges"— certainly by Mendelssohn, but the effect was very distressing. Most producers use the Spring Song and Bee's Wedding as fairy dances, and this effect is quite legitimate and absolutely in the picture with the rest of the score. Mendelssohn is at the top of his form in this music, and here is no Shakespearian Old English Wardour Street style: it is just Mendelssohn at his best, and a very good best it is. With careful arrangement it can be played on a small orchestra, and is a tremendous help to the success of the play. There is bound to be a long wait between the first and second acts—the change from Athens to the Forest—and Weber's overture to *Oberon* is very effective here; and, although scored much more brilliantly than the Mendelssohn music, does not seem out of place, and fills in what would else be a very tiresome interval. Several

English composers have set the fairy chorus, " You spotted snakes," as a glee for mixed voices ; but I never quite fancy fairies singing tenor or bass, and consider Mendelssohn was very wise to stick to women's and children's voices only.

Mendelssohn was only seventeen when he wrote the overture, but the rest of the music was composed much later, at the request of the King of Prussia, and first produced at the New Palace, Potsdam, in 1843. His critical German friends took him much to task for wasting such beautiful music on such a foolish play, but I don't think he ever regretted it. There is a fine ophicleide part in the overture, giving the idea of the clumsy Bottom among the fairies. Mendelssohn chose this instrument because it blends with no other instrument on earth, and really knew what he was doing ; but, because of its very quality of tone, for which he chose it, modern conductors have cut it out and substituted a bass trombone or tuba, both of which blend quite prettily with the other instruments. I am speaking of a few years ago ; there are hardly any ophicleide players left now.

I suppose the great majority of Christians in the world have been " Mendelssohned," as Kipling has it, out of church once in their lives, and I daresay that is why many people talk sniffily about the " Wedding March."

I am going to make a dreadful confession. Once at a small theatre I did the whole of the Mendelssohn music to the *Dream*, excepting the scherzo, on a band of eighteen, and it didn't sound half bad. The parts were carefully cross-cued, and everyone was very busy, but I was very proud of the general effect. Of course, the orchestra was almost beneath the stage, which was a great help. The players—they were picked men—consisted of single wood wind, one horn, two trumpets, one trombone, and drums, four first violins, two second, viola, 'cello, and bass. Incidentally we threw in Weber's *Oberon* overture. I know this sounds like vandalism to read about, but it didn't sound so in the theatre.

Purcell wrote music to a perversion of the *Dream* produced in 1692 (see above, p. 12), and in some strange manner managed not to set a single line of Shakespeare.

John Christopher Smith, composer of an opera called *The Fairies,* founded on *A Midsummer Night's Dream,* was born at Anspach in 1712, but came to England as a boy with his father, who was Handel's treasurer and agent for the sale of his music. At the age of thirteen he became a pupil of Handel, and, when his master went blind, his amanuensis. *The Fairies* was produced in 1754, and on the title-page of the score is written, " the words taken from Shakespeare," but not by whom. Also, unfortunately, as was the manner at the time, the name of the singer is printed, but not that of the character ; however, it is usually possible to get a fairly shrewd idea, from the gist of the words, who is singing. This music is strictly Handelian, though the score as a whole shows greater pains and industry than is generally displayed by his great master. The overture has an introduction, fugue, tuneful minuet, and a fine march in D major after the manner of Handel's *Scipio* march. The first song is for tenor, with trumpet *obbligato*, and, I think, must be intended for Theseus. The words run, " Pierce the air with sounds of joy, Come Hymen with the winged boy, Bring song and dance and revelry." From this I take it that Theseus was preparing for his wedding. It is a very stirring, florid air, and, given a robust tenor and a first-rate trumpeter, makes a good opening for the opera. Helena sings next a song with a very pathetic middle part, saying how she scorns to hide her love. Lysander (baritone) has a brisk song about the joys of country life, followed by Helena, singing, sadly, " O Hermia fair ; O happy, happy fair " ; and Mr Smith sets four lines of Shakespeare's text. Hermia's next air is not very interesting, so we will pass on to a graceful setting of the words, " Love looks not with the eyes, but with the mind," sung by Helena or Hermia, I can't settle which ;

the words are correct text, and very respectfully set. Puck, taken by a boy, now sings, "Where the bee sucks"—quite a new setting to me, and a charming one, too. Here follows an orchestral interlude, called "Sinfonia," for strings, with two independent oboe parts. I don't know if it is meant to be played with the curtain up for business, but rather think it is intended for scene-change music. Titania sings a very "fairy" song, words not by Shakespeare, to her fairies, telling them to follow her; and Oberon, a boy singer, does the same office, in a florid air, for his fairies. Helena, who seems to have too much to do, now has another pathetic song; Titania sings herself to sleep with "You spotted snakes," with slight verbal alterations to make sense. The human lovers become rather tedious here, as they do sometimes in the play; they have several sentimental love-songs and duets, so we welcome Oberon and his fairies. His number, "Now until the break of day," is really beautiful and most fairylike, and brings the second act to a charming close. Oberon sings "Flower of this purple dye" to a solemn *largo* melody, and the mortals take up the tale again. Oberon sings a setting of "Sigh no more, ladies" very interestingly, and sticks closely to the text; it certainly might have been written by Handel, but is none the worse for that. Puck sings "Up and down" to thoroughly suitable music while he chases the foolish lovers about the forest; after which Titania obliges with "Orpheus with his lute," with oboe *obbligato*, quite one of the best numbers in the piece and one of the best settings of these much ill-used lines—the close of the second verse is exquisitely done. A hunting "Sinfonia" heralds the last scene, with a couple of fine solo horn parts. This introduces a bold march for the entrance of Theseus, who has a lusty hunting-song with an elaborate orchestral accompaniment. Hermia now has an unnecessary song, "Love's a tempest," and the opera closes joyfully with a solo and chorus to the words "Hail to love and welcome joy." So ends a work I should very much like to have seen. There is no sign of the clowns in the score, so I fear Smith's librettist cut them out ; but the music is all by one composer and all in one style. There is none of the horrible jostling of periods that annoys one in Bishop's pasticcio Shakespearian operas, and the text is quite as near the original as Bishop's.

If Christopher Smith omitted the clowns, his fellow-countryman, **John Frederick Lampe,** composed a mock-opera, entitled *Pyramus and Thisbe,* the words freely taken from Shakespeare, which was produced at the Theatre Royal, Covent Garden, in 1745.   Johann Friedrich Lampe was born at Helmstadt, Saxony, in 1703.   He came to England as a bassoon player at the opera, and married Isabella Young, a famous singer, sister of Dr Arne's wife.   He soon settled down in London as a composer, and made a tremendous success with his opera *The Dragon of Wantly,* written in imitation of the famous *Beggar's Opera,* and burlesquing current Italian operas.   This Pyramus mock-opera consists of an overture and thirteen numbers.   The overture is a delightfully fresh and original composition, very melodious, with quaint rhythms, and finishing with a very plaintive movement for strings and oboes.   Wall (a tenor) has the first song, words not by Shakespeare, explaining his duties ; it is good burlesque, and great point is made of repeating the word " whispering " seventeen times, making fun of the Italian method of the time somewhat heavily but amusingly.   Pyramus (tenor) has a mock-dignified entrance, and sings an elaborate burlesque song on Shakespeare's words, " And thou, O wall, O sweet and lovely wall, That stands between her father's ground and mine, Show me thy chink that I may blink through with mine eyne."   No other words are used in this long song, and the effect should be very comic, and also irritating to Lampe's contemporaries. Pyramus proceeds with a second song, " O wicked wall," using the last two lines only of his speech in the original text.   Thisbe, the part taken by Mrs Lampe, now enters and sings about her love for Pyramus in a little amorous song, again not by Shakespeare.   The lovers now have a duet, called the First Whispering Duet, to the words, " Not Cephalus to Procris was so true " ; a short spirited duet, " I go without delay," takes them off ; and the Lion enters and roars pleasantly in florid baritone passages. The Moon (tenor) enters and sings of the joys of drinking and loving in the sky. Thisbe has a lament, so well written that it hardly seems a burlesque at all. Pyramus, thinking her dead, sings a furious mock-heroic song, " Approach, ye furies," followed by " Now am I dead," a beautiful plaintive burlesque with *obbligato* parts for two oboes. Thisbe sings her lament, " These lily lips, this cherry nose," to a sad little tune ; however, for some curious reason not explained in the text, neither of the lovers dies, but they finish the burlesque off with a very bright and cheerful duet to the words, " Thus folding, beholding, caressing, possessing, My Thisbe, my dear, We'll live out the year." As there is no spoken dialogue in my copy of this work, I don't know how the author gets over the death of Pyramus and Thisbe : doubtless he has some ingenious way out of it. Some of the fun is quite Shakespearian, and some is very German, but the whole little mock-opera is amusing and worth a few hours' study. The orchestration is simple and good, and the vocal writing, as was nearly always the case in this period, is excellent.

Sir Henry Bishop's operatic version of this play is the first of his series of pasticcio operas founded on Shakespeare's plays. It was produced at the Theatre Royal, Covent Garden, in 1816, and is a wonderful hotch-potch of musical styles from Handel to Bishop. The overture is in four distinct movements, none of which seem to have any bearing on the play or each other ; and not one is used later in the opera. The whole appears to be entirely detached from the rest of the production. The first song (Hermia) is still sometimes heard ; it is by Bishop, and is a melodious setting of the passage beginning " By the simplicity of Venus' doves." The next number is a trio and chorus for the

Clowns, beginning " Most noble Duke." Quince, Snout, and Bottom all have little solos, but I can't trace the words— I think they were by some contemporary of Bishop's ; the tune is by Arne and Bishop, but is not very valuable. The next song is for the first fairy and by Dr Cooke. The words do not occur in the play or in any other work of Shake-speare's ; they are just the conventional fairy-song words about fairy rings, lightly trip it o'er the green, but the musical setting is charming. The fairy march by Bishop is the same as in his *As You Like It*, beginning *pianissimo* and finishing with about fifty bars of such vulgar *fortissimo* noise as would have frightened away any number of fairies. Demetrius has the next song : it is by Bishop, but the words are not Shakespeare's. The words, " But ne'er recall my love," are repeated thirteen times, and the tune is insignificant. The next number is a " grand recitative air and chorus " for Oberon and the fairies ; again the words are not by Shakespeare, but are of the " trip it " and " so nimbly " school ; the music is by Bishop and Dr Cooke, and Cooke's part is the better. Demetrius (tenor) sings Helena's beautiful words, " O happy fair, your eyes are lodestars," to a graceful melody of Bishop's : this number is still heard occasionally. The duet that follows between Demetrius and Hermia is by Bishop, and the words are by Anon. ; it is a maudlin piece of work, words and music admirably fitted. Oberon's beautiful speech, " Flower of the purple dye," is set to music by our old friend Smith, with ineffective additions by Bishop, as a song for Oberon. The second act ends with a recitative for the fourth fairy, a dance and a chorus welcoming the little Indian boy. In the third act is a quartet for the four solo fairies by Bishop, words anonymous and very bad, which takes the curtain up. Oberon sings his speech, " Be as thou wast wont to be," to music by Battishill and Bishop, a very graceful melody ; and this is followed by a hunting chorus about Spartan hounds, music by Bishop, poet unnamed. An anonymous character sings Handel's " Hush, ye pretty warbling choir," from *Acis and Galatea*. The effect should be amazing in this wilderness of bad music. Demetrius now has a song by Bishop, to " original words," called " Sweet cheerful hope," but as it is of no particular value we will pass on to a real piece of Shakespeare from this very play, a setting by Bishop for Oberon and chorus of the words " To the best bride bed will we," finishing with the chorus " In Theseus' house give glimmering light," or, as Shakespeare more happily phrases it, " Through the house," etc. Hermia now sings a song, words by some ruffian unnamed, to Hippolyta and her amazons about freedom; very poor, pretentious stuff. The opera ends with a so-called characteristic march, beginning with the entrance of the Cretans, followed by the Thebans, Amazons, the Centaurs, the Argo, the Labyrinth, the Minotaur—a sort of grand historical pageant of Theseus' life. The music by Bishop is not in the least descriptive of any of these varied things and persons I have catalogued; one expects some rather special music for a Centaur, a Labyrinth, and especially a Minotaur, but one is disappointed.

Mr Cecil Sharp arranged and composed the incidental music and songs for Granville Barker's most interesting production of this play at the Savoy, January 1914. In a striking preface he points out that not a single note of contemporary music for the songs in this play has been preserved; he debates the possibility of using contemporary tunes and fitting the words to them, of having fake music composed, and of commissioning a composer to write entirely new music. He rejects all these propositions, and plumps for using folk-songs. He says: " By using folk-music in the Shakespeare play we shall then be mating like with like, the drama which is for all time with the music which is for all time." Whether the result at the Savoy was successful or not I leave to the judgment of the many people who saw the production. Unfortunately, Mr Sharp does not indicate very clearly when he has arranged, composed, or adapted the tunes in the printed score. The first musical number occurs in Act ii., Scene 2, a dance, song, and chorus ; the dance is to the melody of that interesting old folk-tune " Sellenger's Round," and the baritone solo is, I am sure, by Mr Sharp, as is the following chorus. The words, which fit in too neatly for it to be an adaptation, are the familiar " You spotted snakes " ; but, though he is bitter with Mendelssohn for repeating " so good night " so often, he cheerfully cuts out one " lul-la," surely a grievous thing to do for one so correct ! The next number is Bottom's song, " The ousel cock so black of hue," and is, presumably, by Mr Sharp, as only the melody is printed, and I don't see how anyone can have a copyright (it is marked copyright) in a folk-song tune. I don't think it is an improvement on the so-called traditional tune to which I have always been accustomed. The next number is for orchestra alone, and occurs in Act iv., Scene 1 ; it is called " Still Music," and the melody is the old folk-song, " The sprig of thyme," collected and arranged by Mr Sharp. The Bergamask dance, Act v., Scene 1, is one of the numerous versions of " Green Sleeves," collected and arranged by Mr Sharp. The wedding march is on the tune " Lord Willoughby," arranged by Mr Sharp, and is certainly a great change from the one usually associated with this situation. The love charm seems to have gone all wrong again, and even Theseus and Hippolyta seem to have soured on one another. As for the other lovers—— ! Even the *tierce de Picardie* fails to liven up the last bar. The song and dance in the same scene and act are composed by Mr Sharp, and, following the glorious tradition of Sir Henry Bishop in the pasticcio operas, the words " Roses, their sharp spines being gone " do not appear in the play. They are not by Shakespeare, but from Fletcher's *Two Noble Kinsmen*. The final number is a traditional dance arranged by Mr Sharp, but from what source he does not say ; it is rather a sad little tune, followed by the more lively " Nonsuch," and finishing off with " Sellenger's Round," which was the first musical number.

It would be an interesting point to discover whether Shakespeare would have preferred this very " correct "

musical setting to Mendelssohn's now derided one. I
rather think that Mendelssohn's Overture and Scherzo
would have appealed to him. There seems to me to
be very little in this play, with its frequent classical allu-
sions, that calls for folk-music, and artificial simplicity in
a production of a play so full of Elizabethan artifice
seems utterly out of place.

MUCH ADO ABOUT NOTHING

THE most successful opera founded on *Much Ado About Nothing* is **Berlioz's** two-act work entitled *Béatrice et Bénédict*, produced at Baden, 1862. The composer wrote his own libretto for this, and it is an ingenious one. The first reference we get to the work is in a letter to his greatest friend, Humbert Ferrand, dated November 1858: " I am getting on with a one-act opera for Baden written round Shakespeare's *Much Ado About Nothing*. It is called *Béatrice et Bénédict*; I promise there shall not be ' much ado ' in the shape of noise in it. Benayet, the King of Baden, wants it next year."

A very interesting point is made here in the little joke about " noise." Berlioz had long been accused by critics and public of using too large orchestras. He was very careful to put down in his scores the exact number of each instrument that he required, and the ignorant, non-musical person cannot understand that thirty violins playing *pianissimo* are still *pianissimo* and are infinitely more beautiful than sixteen or eight. Berlioz composed this work, " little opera " he calls it, immensely quickly, and complains that ideas come to him so fast that he has not time to write them down. In a letter to his sailor son, Louis, dated November 1860, he says : " You ask how I manage to crowd a Shakespeare's five acts into one. I have taken only one subject from the play—the part in which Beatrice and Benedick, who detest each other, are mutually persuaded of each other's love, whereby they are inspired with a true passion. The idea is really comic." I don't quite understand what he means by the last sentence : it is certainly a comedy idea, but not to me comic. Perhaps the translation of the original may be somewhat free : I have not the French original version by me, so I quote from the volume in Dent's " Everyman's Library."

It will be noticed that the original idea of a one-act opera is abandoned.   The work was produced in two acts, and was a great success.

Writing again to his son he says: "*Beatrice* was applauded from end to end, and I was recalled more times than I can count " ; and to his friend H. Ferrand : " I am just home from Baden, where *Beatrice* is a real triumph."   He speaks of his " radiant singers."   He says : " People are finding out that I have melody ; that I can be gay—in fact, really comic ; that I am not noisy."   Benayet, whom Berlioz humorously calls " King of Baden," was the director of the new Opera House, and he treated the composer most generously financially, and lavishly as regards scenery and dresses—a thing to which he was not accustomed : so he ennobled him thus.   The whole *Beatrice* episode is one of the happiest in a not very happy life.

Coming to the music itself, the overture is not long, but an admirable comedy overture, beautifully scored.   The first number is a drinking-song in praise of the wine of Syracuse, sung by a bass called Somarone, a creation of Berlioz, with a spirited chorus.

A fine chorus welcomes the return of the victorious Don Pedro.   There is a very pretty " Siciliana," followed by a song in praise of Claudio, sung by Hero.

After this, the hero and heroine have most of the work ; and on their finally agreeing to get married, much simple fun is made by the rest of the characters.   The so-called " Maidens' Duet " became a very popular number.   In this work are two four-part choruses called " Épithalme grotesque," composed in *capella* style.   The end is very bright, and the whole opera though difficult to sing and play, is not expensive to mount.

I cannot trace a performance of this work here in London,

but it would be well worth the attention of the Carl Rosa Opera Company; for even if it has been produced, it must have been a long time ago, and it would be perfectly fresh now. The opera has been performed more frequently in Germany than anywhere else. It was given at Weimar and Stuttgart under the composer's direction, and the last important production was under Mottl.

Sir Charles Villiers Stanford's opera, *Much Ado About Nothing*, has nothing in common with Berlioz's *Béatrice et Bénédict*, and very little in common with Shakespeare's work of the same name. The libretto is by Julian Sturgis, and the work was produced at Covent Garden in May 1900, and also at the Stadt Theater, Leipsic, April 1902, with a German translation by John Bernhoff.

Berlioz took a single episode for his opera in two acts, and worked it out logically, ignoring everything that had nothing to do with his own plot, which was "Beatrice and Benedick." Sturgis and Stanford bring in nearly all Shakespeare's characters, but these say and sing things that would have made Shakespeare turn in his grave if he could have heard them there. When Debussy wanted to set Maeterlinck's *Pelléas et Mélisande*, he set every word of the original play and made a perfect work of art. When Richard Strauss made an opera of Oscar Wilde's *Salome*, he did the same thing, and, however much some of us may dislike it, no one can deny that he turned out a very perfect art-work, as regards form and brilliance. He produced a great opera, unpleasant from some points of view, but, judged as a whole, a real achievement. He trusted in his librettist and was justified in his trust. Stanford did not trust in Shakespeare as much as he did in Julian Sturgis, and his trust was very much betrayed.

Touching on the opera purely from a musical point of view, there is much very pleasant music in it. There is no overture, and the first act begins just before the masque. The male chorus sings "Sigh no more, ladies" as the curtain rises.

Almost at once Don John and Borachio begin the plot. Claudio and Benedick enter, Claudio immediately disclosing his love for Hero, the story of the play being pretty closely followed. Leonato now makes a tardy effort to welcome Don Pedro and the rest, and a masque begins with a very stately saraband. Then, according to stage directions, " Enter a pomp of clowns and country girls," who dance a morris-dance, while the chorus sings about spring and maying. The masque ends with Hero, crowned Queen of Summer, singing a very graceful welcome to the princes. Claudio, as in Shakespeare, thinks the prince is wooing for himself, and sings a tragic farewell to Hero and love, with many repetitions of the words " farewell " and " love." Beatrice and Benedick then have their little comedy scene, and the Prince explains to Claudio that he has won Hero for him, and gives him some solemn advice. All the principals join in and sing a fine sextet, Don John on the bottom line singing with the others, but with sinister significance, that he will mar their music presently.

The Prince announces his intention of making Beatrice and Benedick fall in love with each other, and the four conspirators, Hero, Claudio, Pedro, and Leonato, sing a quartet about it, finishing with a great number of " with a fa-la-la's." Don John says he will cross the wedding, and in a few words tells Borachio to meet Hero's gentle-woman, Margaret, that night, and he will bring the Prince and Claudio. The doors of the supper-room are thrown open and a procession of guests comes out, with Hero and Claudio in the centre, the chorus singing " Sigh no more, ladies," until the curtain comes down on the first act.

The second act opens with a short orchestral introduction. The scene is Leonato's garden near Hero's window. Claudio sings a typical serenade, at the end of which Hero comes out on the balcony, and they have a long love-duet. Benedick then enters, and sings a lengthy and very clever soliloquy about love and ladies; and then Hero, Pedro, and Claudio, in a vocal trio, describe the love of Beatrice for

Benedick, the last-named listening as in the play. The scene ends with a very bright trio by the conspirators about having snared their bird.

The next episode sticks closely to Shakespeare. Don John guides Pedro and Claudio to Hero's window; they see Borachio embrace Margaret, and Claudio makes up his mind to denounce Hero in the church. The act ends excitedly by Claudio rushing off, followed by Don Pedro and Don John, and the curtain quickly falls.

The third act opens tempestuously on the orchestra, typifying Claudio's bitter thoughts. He is discovered alone in the church, where he sings a grim and very dramatic quasi-recitative about Hero's fall from grace. The bells are now heard—only three, F, G, A, and the organ begins, acolytes lighting the altar candles. The church fills, friars start the hymn outside to the words, " Mater dulce carmen lenis," the bells going right through the hymn with excellent effect. Then comes Claudio's denunciation of Hero and his refusal to marry her ; she swoons, and everyone leaves the church except Hero, Beatrice, Benedick, Leonato, and the friar. The friar, in a fine bass number (beautifully sung at Covent Garden by Pol Plançon), explains his plan of pretending that Hero has died of shame at the false accusation. Benedick promises to challenge Claudio, and during this scene a funeral bell is heard, and a procession of the Misericordia Fraternity crosses the stage carrying a bier and singing " Miserere mei Deus " as it passes out of sight. Benedick sings very solemnly " And so farewell " (I don't quite see why, because Benedick knows Hero is not dead), and the curtain comes down to *fortissimo* music on a very effective third act.

The last act takes place in Messina, near the burial-ground of Leonato's family. The music to open is not at all gloomy, as it is to introduce Seacole, Dogberry, and Verges. Curiously enough, Verges is a silent performer, or, as he is called in the bill of the play, a " persona muta." The watch come straight to the point. They have caught Borachio telling of his doings, and the movement follows

very closely Shakespeare's development of the episode.
Benedick comes on, tries to make a song in Beatrice's
honour, fails (just as he did in Shakespeare), but finally
sings quite a good song about "Morning, spring-a (*sic*)
ring-a (*sic*) and chantecleer." Don Pedro and Claudio
enter; Benedick delivers his challenge and they prepare
to fight, when Don Pedro comes between them. Dogberry,
Verges, Watchmen with Borachio, bound, enter, and all
the villainy of Don John is explained. The Friar enters;
Claudio begs forgiveness, and the Friar produces the living
Hero without any of Shakespeare's pretence that she was
another daughter. Claudio at once sings a song to Hero,
calling her angel of pity, and sentimentalising over her for
quite a long time. Hero joins in the general soppiness,
and, after a great high-note effect on the part of both,
Beatrice and Benedick break in with their comedy scene,
in which they agree to get married, to shouts of "How
dost thou, Benedick, the married man!" The principals
and chorus all join in singing "Sigh no more, ladies,"
which finally brings down the curtain very brightly on a
charming comedy opera; the music vastly superior to
the book. It was a brave attempt of Sir Charles Stanford,
but he was beaten by his librettist every time. It is not
my intention to give Mr Sturgis's perversions of Shakespeare; but why not have followed the original text
whenever possible, and cut anything that would have made
the work too long? Some of the paraphrases are quite
as long as the original, but how lamentably weak! If
only Sturgis had used Shakespeare and a large blue
pencil! Of course, the whole text is too long to set for
an opera—even as a play it is too long; but to rewrite
immortal phrases and put them into such obvious opera
libretto form (of the worst period) was a foolish thing to do,
and will kill Stanford's heroic attempt to achieve English
grand opera whenever it is performed. Mr Sturgis touched
no phrase of Shakespeare's that he did not degrade; there
is really no reason why the libretto of a modern opera
should be written in rhyming couplets.

There are two other operas on this subject, but neither has yet been performed in England : *Beaucoup de Bruit pour Rien*, by **P. Puget** (Paris, 1899) ; and *Ero*, by **C. Podesta** (Cremona, 1900), about the latter of which I regret I can obtain no details.   The former, an opera in four acts and five scenes, libretto taken from Shakespeare's play by Edouard Blau, music by Paul Puget, was first performed at the Opéra Comique, Paris, on March 24, 1899. As a whole, the librettist adheres closely to his text, with the exception of the omission of Dogberry and Verges ; and I don't think that anyone except an Englishman could possibly understand two such thoroughly British characters.   In this work they would only make the serious parts seem ridiculous.   The last scene of the last act is novel, and owes very little to Shakespeare.   Hero is lying on a mortuary bed before the altar of the cathedral ; Claudio enters, throws open the great doors, and, in the presence of all, makes a humble confession of his mistake and begs for pardon.   He swears to consecrate himself to her, and puts on her finger a ring.   At the touch of his hand Hero comes slowly from her faint, and the piece finishes happily.   It is a very good libretto, and quite as near the original text as an opera can be expected to be. To this libretto M. Puget has composed some very beautiful music.   The prelude to the first act is full of happy characterisation, though rather short.   The duet, Hero and Beatrice, sung while they present flowers to Don Pedro, is melodious and simple ; and in this act there is a very pretty Sicilian song and dance.   In the second act a madrigal, sung by Benedick, is charming and very delicately scored, as is also a quartet for Pedro, Leonato, Benedick, and Beatrice.   In the third act, the scene of the arrival of the bridal cortege at the cathedral, with fine organ and orchestral effects, is very impressive ; and in the last scene, the long monologue, addressed by Claudio to the crowd, is broadly phrased and very pathetic in its dignity : but it is unfortunately largely overscored.   The one serious blot on the work is the tendency of the composer to over-

weight the singers.   The opera earned a very well-deserved
success.

Edward German's overture and incidental music for
Sir George Alexander's production of *Much Ado* at the
St James's, 1898, is German at his best.   The overture is
mostly very bright, the first theme being really a saltarello.
The second *motif*, Hero and Claudio, is naturally more
sentimental and subdued.   Don Pedro has a fine theme
(the third subject of the overture), which is afterwards
used for his entrance.   These themes are all blended and
woven together, and the whole ends with a brilliant coda,
in saltarello style again.   There is a very pretty movement,
alla Siciliana, called " Leonato's Garden " ; while the Dogberry music is in a hurried, flurried manner, quite indicating the fussy old constable.   The Bourrée and Gigue are
very well known on the concert platform.   The former is
one of the prettiest Old English dances that Edward
German has ever given us.   The *grandioso* effect of the
first theme coming in augmentation for the coda is wonderfully good, and makes a really brilliant ending.   In the
Gigue, also, German is in his happiest vein ; but I fear that
a great deal of the incidental music is still in manuscript.

OTHELLO

Rossini's *Otello*, produced at Naples, 1816, is the earliest grand opera on the subject. For many years it enjoyed great popularity. But in 1887, in Milan, was produced Verdi's tragic masterpiece, and the earlier composer's work died a very natural death.

Many serious critics have said that Verdi's is the great tragedy opera of the world, but, anyhow, it is a great tragic opera. The incidental music composed for stage productions of the play has never been of very much importance. There is supposed to be a traditional setting of the "Willow Song," sung by Desdemona; but, as Shakespeare did not even write the words of the said song, merely quoting a few lines from a long poem given in its entirety by Bishop Percy in his invaluable *Reliques*, this setting, even if contemporary, has not much to do with our subject, "Shakespeare and Music." The other songs, "King Stephen was a worthy peer," and "Let me the canakin clink, clink," are both probably quotations from older songs; while the so-called "traditional" tunes are very like the so-called "traditional" etc. in other plays by the master. In point of fact, I have often heard an old actor sing the King Stephen lyric to the same tune as the First Gravedigger's song in *Hamlet*, and the two bear a very close resemblance to the traditional tune of "The Babes in the Wood." Still, the so-called traditional (I am tired of writing the word) setting of "A poor soul sat sighing" is a very exquisite thing, and worthy of its place in any production of the play. But the purity of its *melodic line* would probably stand out in contrast to its modern associates, if introduced into a modern version of the incidental music ; so it is as well to leave it honourably alone, and write a new setting more in keeping with the rest of one's music.

Dvořák's fine *Othello* overture is fairly well known in concert-halls, but is too long and elaborate for theatre use. It is scored for full orchestra with harp, and an important part for English horn. The opening is slow and *pianissimo*, muted strings giving out an almost hymn-like subject, occasionally broken in upon by anticipation of the real principal theme. This is developed very dramatically, and leads skilfully into the first subject proper—a very quick, bright, one-in-a-bar theme, with tragic suggestions in it.

The second subject is of a more peaceful character, and the work slows down for a while. The long development is mostly very strenuous, but just before the end are some beautiful sad passages full of tragedy and pathos. The end is *fortissimo* and *accelerando*, with a curious sequence of passing notes in the melody against a very rough chord, repeatedly struck by the rest of the orchestra. Though a little long, this overture is full of dramatic and melodic interest, and is, so far as I know, the only composition directly founded on our dramatist by this composer.

Raff's "Othello" overture is a fine though uninspired work.

Rossini's grand three-act opera, *Otello*, libretto by the Marquis Berio, enjoyed a long run of popularity. It was first produced at the Teatro del Fondo in the autumn of 1816. Originally Othello, Roderigo, and Iago were all great tenor parts; but later, Rossini, realising the difficulty of getting three tenors of high standing to sing together, rewrote the part of Iago for baritone.

The work made an enormous impression, and was soon being played over all Europe. In many ways it was much in advance of its time, the composer writing his own ornaments and embellishments, and often successfully investing them with real dramatic meaning. In the last act the librettist introduces a new character who sings a barcarolle to Dante's celebrated words, " Nessun maggior dolore." This is one of the most beautiful things in the work. It is for tenor. The librettist does not attempt to adapt Shakespeare's tragedy, but is content to take enough plot and situations for a conventional Italian libretto, and he succeeds in doing this very well.

The overture is studiously conventional, but some of the numbers are very beautiful. The duet between Desdemona and Emilia, " Vorrei che il tuo pensiero," is strikingly lovely ; and the quintet in the finale of the first act is a fine piece of writing, the insistently-recurring ascending scale of Brabantio to the words " il barbaro tenor " having a terrific effect. The duet, Othello and Iago, in the second act, is full of melodic beauty and dramatic moments. Desdemona's great aria, " Assisa a piè d'un salice," is really beautiful, and the end of the opera is truly dramatic. The whole work is unquestionably Rossini's greatest opera, with the exception of *William Tell*.

Verdi's " lyrical drama in four acts," book by Arrigo Boito, is on a very different plane. Here we have the finest opera-librettist, with the possible exception of Richard Wagner, collaborating with one of the greatest dramatic composers of all time on a subject by the dramatist of all time—and a stupendous work is the result.

The comparative slowness of the sung as against the spoken word has necessitated much cutting, but with great technical skill Boito has devised a wonderful book, as true to Shakespeare as is possible in a libretto. The work was first produced at the Scala, Milan, February 5, 1887. The English translation is by Francis Hueffer, for a long time musical critic of the *Times*. The success was immediate, and the opera at once passed into the world-repertory.

There is no overture, and the whole action of the piece

takes place in Cyprus. In the original production Tamagno and Maurel were Othello and Iago. After two and a half bars of *fortissimo* orchestral music, the curtain rises on a tavern with an arbour. In the background is the sea. It is night, and a storm is raging. It is really Shakespeare's Act ii., Scene 1. Iago, Cassio, Montano, Roderigo, and chorus are watching Othello's ship, buffeting the waves, making slowly for harbour. Eventually Othello lands, and explains that the ocean has overwhelmed the Turk, and the war is over. Othello goes into the castle, and the chorus celebrate the happy news, the storm gradually dying away. No finer opening for an opera has ever been devised, and it is remarkable how the composer and librettist have managed to sustain this high level right through the four acts of the work.

Iago and Roderigo, following closely the original text, conspire against Othello, and the crowd make a bonfire in the background. Cassio enters and joins a group of soldiers, and the crowd light the bonfire and sing a chorus in praise of fire generally ; at the end of which Iago tempts Cassio to drink, and sings an enlargement of " And let me the canakin clink," the chorus joining in the refrain.

Cassio gets very drunk, and the Shakespeare text is closely followed. Towards the end of the fight Othello has a magnificent entrance. He stops the strife with the words, " Lay down your arms."

After a tremendous *fortissimo* chord on the orchestra there is a long and most significant pause. Then Othello has a beautiful but most distressing scene with Cassio. All exit save Desdemona and Othello, who sing an exquisite and passionate love-duet, which finishes the first act.

Near the beginning of the second act Iago has his first long soliloquy : very grim, but most dramatic. The duet between Othello and Iago that follows, in which Iago sows the seeds of jealousy, carries the action forward swiftly, and the " green-ey'd monster " lines are impressively set. At the close of the scene a chorus is heard singing softly, " off," accompanied by two notes (tonic and dominant) on the cornamusa, or "bay-pipes." Grove is silent on the subject of the cornamusa; but Riemann, in his *Dictionary of Music*, says it is "an old Italian kind of schalmey," "also similar to the word bagpipe": so that "bay-pipe" is obviously a misprint for bagpipe in my edition of this work. The schalmey or schalmei was the predecessor of the oboe. This accompaniment is added to by mandolins and guitars on the stage, and gradually the whole orchestra joins in. The chorus is peaceful and melodious, and makes a strong dramatic contrast to what has gone before and what follows. At the end of this chorus Desdemona intercedes with Othello in Cassio's favour, and really fans the flame of jealousy; Othello denounces Desdemona, and the act ends with a dramatic duet between Othello and his betrayer.

The third act has a somewhat longer orchestral prelude than the first two, but the librettist gets to work very swiftly none the less. The handkerchief business is immediately begun. A long duet between Desdemona and Othello follows, the former very loving, the latter very ironical, the whole culminating in a magnificent passage in which Othello sings the words, " I mistook you . . . for that strumpet of Venice who has married Othello." Desdemona is overwhelmed with horror, and Othello pushes her out of the room. There is great trumpeting from all sides of the stage, and, to a chorus of welcome by the Cypriotes, the Venetian ambassadors enter, bringing Othello's letter of recall. After a big chorus and ensemble, Othello and his ancient are left alone ; the former gets more and more excited, and finally swoons. Iago jeers at the fallen Othello, the chorus, behind, sings "Hail, Othello," and on this situation, to a great music of trumpets, the curtain falls.

The fourth act opens with a short orchestral prelude on the subject of the " Willow Song," which comes a little later. The scene is Desdemona's bedroom, and she and Emilia are discovered. After a short dialogue, Desdemona sings the " Willow Song." For sheer beauty this is the most exquisite thing in the work : it is a wonderful piece of pure lyrical writing. Emilia says " Good night," and exits. Desdemona intones to a sustained accompaniment a " Hail, Mary," and then sings a beautiful prayer. She lies down on the bed, and long-sustained high chords are heard on the orchestra. These cease, and a sinister motive on the lowest bass notes is heard *pianissimo*. At the first note Othello is seen standing on the threshold of a secret door. To a certain musical figure he lays his scimitar on the table. He stands before the candle, doubtful whether to blow it out or not ; he goes to the bed ; he stops himself ; he raises the curtains and looks for a long time at the sleeping Desdemona ; he kisses her once, again, again, and she wakens. It must be understood that until Desdemona wakens not a word is spoken, but the whole action is fitted to the most dramatic and speaking music, and the effect is awe-inspiring. He tells her to pray, as he does not want to kill her soul; and after a short duet he stifles her, and she utters a shriek. This arouses Emilia, who knocks three times on the door—Othello still gazing at Desdemona—three times again, and yet again. Each knock is as carefully written down in the score as if it were a part for a musical instrument—Verdi is so thorough. Finally Othello opens the door. Desdemona manages to gasp out, " I have been slain unjustly, I die here guiltless," and expires. Emilia shouts for help, and Ludovico, Cassio, Iago, and others enter. All is explained to the unfortunate Othello, who suddenly stabs himself. As he is dying he sings the perfect words, " I kissed thee ere I killed thee ;— no way but this, Killing myself, to die upon a kiss." Mr Hueffer has slightly altered the last six words, but I have ventured to put back Shakespeare's original text ; in fact, I could not have put down the translator's variant. On these immortal words, sung *pianissimo*, the curtain falls on this great art-work.

The perfect combination of Verdi and Boito, and the sympathy of both with Shakespeare, are amongst the wonders of the world to me. The art of collaboration has never, to my knowledge, been brought to such a pitch of perfection except in the case of *Falstaff*, the work of the same trio. George Meredith, in one of his letters, dated 1896, with reference to his friend Professor W. G. Plimmer, a well-known amateur musician, writes : " He has got a score of *Othello* to play to me ; says it is Wagner and water ; would seem to say it is Verdi-gris of Wagner " ; which shows that the Professor may have been some sort of a musician, but was certainly an amateur. Some critics endeavour to trace the influence of Wagner on Verdi's later operas, but I think it was the composer's own rich development in his later years that made his last two operas stand out so much from the rest of his operatic work. Of course, Wagner's influence on his contemporaries, especially the younger ones, was, and is still, enormous in Germany. But though it is quite easy to trace the harmonic and melodic influence of Wagner on Humperdinck or Strauss, I quite fail to see either influence on Verdi. The two operas are the natural result of a glorious old age.

Arnold Krug, born 1849 at Hamburg, has written an interesting symphonic prologue to this play. After the usual slow introduction, we start away with a good, quick, syncopated theme for strings, soon added to by wood wind (evidently the fiery Othello). Then comes the gentle Desdemona theme, which persists for a long time, after which the music gets really exciting. Iago works Othello up to a frenzy of jealousy ; Desdemona's gentle explanations are overborne. After a strong climax her end comes, followed shortly afterwards by Othello's. The coda is a short *morendo* episode, in the major, and very peaceful.

Though this work is by no manner of means great, it is not without interest, and it is one of the few purely abstract compositions we have on this play.

Zdenko Fibich, who has composed a very interesting symphonic poem on the theme, was a leader of the " Young Czech " musical movement. He was born on December 21, 1850, at Seborschity, near Tschlau, and was taught music at Prague and Leipsic. This is his first symphonic poem, but it is a very interesting example of the composer's method.

Though there is no definite programme, Fibich quotes several passages from the play to indicate his intentions. The first is :—

> . . . Rude am I in my speech,
> And little bless'd with the set phrase of peace.

Here there is a fanfare for trumpets and horns working into a strong, rough military march. Music descriptive of Othello's many adventures follows, until he says :—

> This only is the witchcraft I have us'd—
> Here comes the lady ; let her witness it.

Then the Desdemona melody, oboe solo, harp, and strings, makes its appearance. This is really a beautiful theme, perfectly orchestrated, and it just expresses Desdemona's character. Her words, written in the score, are : " I saw Othello's visage in his mind ; And to his honours and his valiant parts Did I my soul and fortunes consecrate." Presently comes Iago with his " jealousy " *motif*, which struggles for a long time with Desdemona's " innocent " theme, but finally wins. The music is intensely dramatic here : the clash of wills, Iago's and Othello's, and the sweet personality of Desdemona, all struggling for predominance. Finally the trombone and tuba blaze out, *fortissimo* and *grandioso*, the jealousy theme in octaves. The music dies away, and for the last time the Desdemona melody is heard very *piano*. Four short, violently *forte* bars follow (the brass having the theme), and the work ends with a solo *pianissimo* chord on the harp. The end is most curious, such an immense amount of meaning being got into the last fifteen bars. The whole work makes a fine piece of vivid orchestral tone-painting, and the music distinctly derives from Shakespeare's text, and is worthy of it. The last words quoted are Othello's : " I kissed thee ere I killed thee ;—no way but this, Killing myself, to die upon a kiss."

8

Sir Herbert Tree commissioned **Samuel Coleridge Taylor**
to write the music for his revival of *Othello* at His
Majesty's.   The composer has made a suite for orchestra
out of the numbers written for this production.   The first
section is called just a Dance.   This is strictly Oriental in
character, full of movement and excitement.   The second
number is a " Children's Intermezzo," and is very simple
in character.   No touch of the Orient here.   No. 3 is
a Funeral March in G minor, mostly written on two ground
basses, one for the march and one for the trio.   It is a fine
broad movement, working up to a great climax in the
middle and dying away very effectively afterwards.   The
setting of the famous " Willow Song " is simple and
beautiful.

KING RICHARD III

The play of *Richard III.* has not attracted musicians. I can only trace one opera founded on it—that by the French composer, **Gervais Bernard Salvayre,** produced 1883 at Petrograd. This work was a dead failure, its chief faults—noisiness and an amalgamation of different styles, from Meyerbeer to Verdi—being so prominent that it was only performed a few times. Concerning two other works, which I have not been able to find, a few bare *data* are given below.

Of incidental music, specially composed, much has been written, but most of it is unimportant. Many producers seem to have been content with a funeral march and a liberal use of fanfares; but the late Richard Mansfield, the Anglo-American actor-manager, had the good sense to commission **Edward German** to compose the music for his production at the Globe in 1889, and the result is a fine overture and some very effective and appropriate incidental music.

The overture is in strict form. It opens *maestoso,* the Richard III. theme being given out *forte.* It is a sinister subject, well suited to the character Shakespeare drew, if not in agreement with our modern whitewashing historians. After this short introduction the overture proper starts, with Richard's *motif* on the violins, *allegro molto,* accompanied by *tremolo* strings. This is worked up to a fine *fortissimo,* and prepares the way for the second theme, "The Princes." Here we have a tender melody, again suited to the author's picture of the characters, but not at all like the horrible little prigs one generally sees in these parts in the theatre. Personally I have every sympathy with Richard for killing the Princes whenever I see them on the stage ! This theme is worked up to a fine climax, and then the very clever development begins. The subjects are well mixed and blended, and the overture comes to an end in a very brilliant manner.

In the incidental music the first number is the King Henry theme, a plaintive minor melody ; then the Lady Anne *motif*, also plaintive, but not minor. The Lord Mayor theme is a mock dignified march, marked "quaintly" in the score. The number called " On the Way to Chertsey " is in the " Old English style," and foreshadows the famous " Henry VIII. Dances " that followed. " In the Tower " is naturally sombre, very ominous and fateful. The " Entrance of the young Duke of York " is a pretty, boyish, scherzo-like little number ; and " In Baynard Castle " is a serious, organ-like piece of music all on a pedal, and rather like a conventional postlude. " Richmond's March " is also serious, and is marked " religioso," an allusion to his well-known habit of praying !

The processional march, played as Queen Elizabeth and train enter the Tower, is a fine, pompous, thoroughly English march, as is fitting for the occasion ; and the " Intermezzo Funèbre," played as King Henry's funeral procession approaches, is all its name promises. The work ends with a short " Victory theme." This score, which was the first incidental music written by Edward German, then musical director at the Globe, made quite a sensation, and abundantly justified Mansfield's selection of his composer.

Frederick Smetana, born March 2, 1824, perhaps the greatest Bohemian musician, wrote a great symphonic poem on this play. It is a very elaborate work and laid out for a very large orchestra. The composer gives no definite programme, but the music throughout is very dramatic and full of tragic interest. After a few quiet introductory bars the basses give out the principal theme quietly, but working quickly up to a *fortissimo*.

This subject, with slight changes, dominates the entire work ; it is a grim, characteristic, sinister theme, and a splendid one to develop. Almost immediately it has been announced the answering *motif*, plaintive and melodious, follows, and for a long time these are the only subjects used. After a good working-up, a four-note figure of the theme is taken by itself and developed into a great march tune, typical of the King in his pomp. After this, one new subject is introduced—a breathless, syncopated, *agitato* phrase, which, worked up with the other theme, develops into a magnificent coda, marked " vittorioso " in the score— victory for Richmond, I suppose. The last few bars are again grim, the same four notes from Richard's theme broken in upon by two sharp *fortissimo* chords.

This is indeed a welcome addition to our scanty stock of *Richard III*. music. It is a symphonic poem in the grand manner, and worthy to stand with the greatest works in that class. This work was first performed in England at the first Henschel concert, St James's Hall, November 12, 1896.

All that is known of an opera bearing the impressive title of *Ricardus Impius, Angliæ Rex, ab Henrico Richmondæ Comite vita simul et regno exitus*, is that it was a drama in Latin, music by Jean d'Eberlin, and was produced by the students of the Benedictine convent at Salzburg on September 4, 1750. The composer, **Johann Ernst Eberlin,** was born at Jettingen, Bavaria, 1702, and died at Salzburg, Austria, in 1762. He was Court organist to the Prince Bishop of the latter town, and chief organist to the Cathedral. He composed an immense amount of church and organ music.

The other work unknown to me is **Canepa's** *Riccardo III*. (Milan, 1879).

ROMEO AND JULIET

IT is a curious fact that, though *Romeo and Juliet* contains more exquisite lyrical passages than almost any other play of Shakespeare, there is no song or lyric in it.

Anyone except Romeo would have hired a quartet, or anyway one singer, to serenade Juliet under her balcony; but she remains unserenaded. Even the four lines beginning " When griping grief " (sung by Peter in Act iv., Scene 4) are not Shakespeare's, but quoted by him from Richard Edwards's *Paradise of Daintee Devices*, and sung to a so-called traditional tune. But if there is no song like " Sigh no more, ladies," or " Who is Sylvia ? ", there is little doubt that a greater number of composers have been inspired (more or less) by this tragedy than by any other of Shakespeare's subjects if we except *Hamlet*. A mere list of the names is imposing. The most popular work is, no doubt, **Gounod's** opera *Roméo et Juliette*. The book, which adheres fairly closely to the original play, is by Barbier and Carré, and the work was first performed at the Lyrique, Paris, on April 27, 1867. The characters are the same as those of Shakespeare's play, with the addition of Stephano, page to Romeo (mez. sop.), and Gregorio, a watchman. The waltz in Act i. is a very popular *coloratura* soprano song, but is not in the least the kind of thing the real Capulet would have allowed the real Juliet to sing to his guests. Mercutio's Queen Mab scene is very effective, as are the Balcony duet and the prelude to the fifth act. But the most successful and to my mind the most Shakespearian character in the whole opera is Friar Laurence, a conception full of dignity and pathos. Pol Plançon was magnificent in this part. Taken altogether, Gounod has turned out a very successful French grand opera, which will hold its place in opera repertories for many years to come.

The only other opera on this story that has had any great success is **Bellini's** work in three acts, *I Capuletti ed i Montecchi*, book by Romani, produced at Venice, March 11, 1830. It is a real Bellini, full of florid arias, word repetitions, bravura passages, cadenzas, and all the vocal gymnastics so beloved of his period; but the music, as a whole, would fit any story quite as badly as it does that of Romeo and Juliet. The overture is rather curious. The first subject, second subject, development, recapitulation, and coda are all in the same key, that of D major. The effect is overwhelming. It is a perfect tonic orgy. An amusing account of this opera is given by Berlioz in his *Autobiography*. During the time he held the Prix de Rome, passing through Florence, he heard some strangers at a *table d'hôte* talking of Bellini's *Montecchi*, which was soon to be given. He writes : " Not only did they praise the music, but also the libretto. Italians as a rule care so little for the words of an opera that I was surprised, and thought—at last I shall hear an opera worthy of that glorious play. What a subject it is ! Simply made for music. The ball at Capulet's house, where young Romeo first sees his dearly loved one; the street fight at which Tybalt presides, patron of anger and revenge; that indescribable night-scene at Juliet's balcony; the witty sallies of Mercutio; the prattle of the Nurse; the solemnity of the Friar trying to soothe the conflicting elements ; the awful catastrophe; and the reconciliation of the rival families over the bodies of the ill-fated lovers. I hurried to the Pergola Theatre. What a disappointment! No ball, no Mercutio, no babbling Nurse, no balcony scene, no Shakespeare ! And Romeo sung by a small thin *woman*, Juliet by a tall stout one. Why, in the name of all things musical—why ? "

I will just enumerate the remainder of the operatic settings, giving date and place of production and names of composer and librettist. It is rather a formidable list, but one never hears any of the works mentioned, save those of Steibelt and Vaccaj, at the outside; and as for Bellini's version, it would scarcely be possible to hear it anywhere out of Italy.

Romeo e Giulietta, a serious opera in three acts, by **Zingarelli,** was composed in Milan and first performed in that city (1796). It was produced in Paris in 1812, and had some success. Nicolò Antonio Zingarelli was born in Naples, 1752. He was celebrated in his lifetime, and was thought much of by Haydn, who prophesied a great career for him. According to Coppa, his librettist, he wrote the opera in " forty hours less than ten days." He composed a cantata for the Birmingham Festival of 1829, and, as he could not take it to England himself, entrusted it to his pupil Costa. This was Michael Costa's first introduction to the English public. Hence the Philharmonic pitch and loud orchestral playing from which we suffered for so many years. The two most celebrated numbers in the opera are the duet " Dunque mio ben " for soprano and contralto, and the air " Ombra adorata aspetta." The Emperor Napoleon I. was unable to hide his emotion when he heard this song, especially when sung by Crescentini (Romeo) ; who achieved so great a success with this melody that he persuaded himself that he was the real composer. This fable obtained, very unjustly, some credence from the general public. The last time the Emperor heard Crescentini sing this song he was so affected that he sent him from his own breast the Order of the Iron Crown, and gave the composer an order for a Mass for the Imperial Chapel that should not last longer than twenty minutes. He had it rehearsed in his presence, and was so pleased that he gave the musician 6000 francs. Zingarelli was an enormously productive composer, and wrote a great number of operas, as well as quantities of church and chamber music, but one seldom hears his name now. His music is still sung in provincial Catholic churches.

Roméo et Juliette, an opera in three acts, book by M. de Ségur, music by **Daniel Steibelt**, was produced at the Théâtre Feydeau, 1793, just four months after the production of a work on the same subject by Monnel and Dalayrac, *All for Love*, or *Roméo et Juliette*. In spite of this clashing, the opera was a success. It had been refused by the Academy of Music, so the authors cut the recitatives, put in prose dialogue, and produced the piece as an *opéra comique*. The *Moniteur* of September 23 describes the music as " learned, but laboured and ugly." However, the public loved it, and other critics say it had power and originality and distinguished voluptuous melody. Juliette's song, " The calm of the night," and the quartet, " Graces, virtues," held their own for a long time ; as did the funeral chorus at the end of the second act.

In 1825, at the Théâtre Italien de Paris, in Milan, **Nicolò Vaccaj** produced his opera on the same subject. It is one of the composer's best efforts, the finest scene being that at the tomb. The air, " Ah, se tu dormi svegliati," is pathetic and passionate. The last act of this work is often substituted for the last act of the Bellini opera already dealt with, as the latter composer's fourth act is very weak. Nicolò Vaccaj was born at Tolentino in 1790. He spent some years in London, where he was a very successful singing teacher. He wrote a great amount of music, but none of it is very distinguished.

The **Marquis Richard d'Ivry** composed an opera on this subject, produced in Paris in 1878. He was a gifted amateur, born, February 4, 1829, at Beaune (Côte-d'Or), and composed several other operas. This one was dedicated to Edward VII. when he was Prince of Wales, and was called *Les Amants de Vérone*, a lyric drama in five acts, words and music by d'Ivry. The music, not at all ambitious, is tuneful and simple. The most important number is the farewell duet between Romeo and Juliet in the second act. A critic, writing of this work, says : " It is a pity that the author has not corrected in his poem those vulgar expressions that disfigure it, and in his music those old-fashioned formulas (*peu nouvelles*)." As I have only the piano solo copy before me, I cannot speak on the first complaint ; but on the second I agree with the critic. The work is amateurish and old-fashioned, often in the abusive sense of the word, but it is certainly melodious and generally unpretentious. Each act has quite a pretty and effective prelude, and the occasional dances are graceful.

Pietro Carlo Guglielmi's opera on this play, *Romeo e Giulietta*, was produced in London in 1810. The composer was born at Naples in 1763. There are several detached numbers in the British Museum Library. They are just the ordinary Italian opera music of the time. The wonder of the story does not seem to have made the slightest impression on the composer, who proceeds calmly on his conventional way, after one interesting burst of originality : he actually makes Romeo a bass baritone ! After this one is not so surprised to find Juliet a deep mezzo, nearly a contralto. To make up for the lack of tenor interest, the part of Paris is made quite important, and among other numbers he is given a very effective duet with Juliet. One of Juliet's songs is described as " The Favourite Prayer," and is quite a good example of the conventional operatic music of the period ; as is Romeo's song with chorus, in which he strives to quiet the street-quarrel between the rival houses. The love duets with Juliet are thoroughly vocal ; and the trios, called " Favourite " again, for the lovers and the Friar, and for Bianca and the lovers, are pretty melodious stuff, but utterly lacking any sense of drama.

Of the non-operatic works on this subject, **Berlioz's** symphony *Romeo and Juliet* is by far the greatest.

During the six years that Hector Berlioz was a student at the Paris Conservatoire, the two influences that affected him and his work most, according to his own memoirs, were those of William Shakespeare and Ludwig van Beethoven. It is interesting and strange that perhaps the greatest of all French musicians should have been so profoundly moved by the plays of an English poet and the music of a Dutch musician. I speak of Beethoven here intentionally as Dutch, because his father was Dutch, and had only lived in Germany two years when Beethoven was born; and I consider that a man takes his nationality from his father and not from his actual birthplace. Beethoven could certainly have played cricket for the Rhineland on a strict birth qualification; but he was distinctly of Dutch blood, and took the precaution of leaving Germany for Austria as soon as he could. Finally came another influence to drive Berlioz further into the arms of Shakespeare but not of Beethoven—also a foreign one, that of Henrietta Smithson, the Irish actress. She was playing Shakespeare heroines at the Odéon early in 1833. He fell madly in love with her and went to see her whenever she played, just as our modern gilded youths haunt the stalls every night to see their favourite musical-comedy actress; the only difference being that Berlioz saw his dear one in many different and exquisite characters, while our youths hear their favourites say the same few lines or sing the same little song every night of the year. Berlioz composed music for her and gave concerts of his own compositions in her honour (the latter must have bored her very much, judging from the attitude of the average actress towards serious music— and Miss Smithson, from all accounts, was not a great actress); and finally he married her. They lived together as unhappily as possible for several years, and then parted; but at least one great art work was the result of their union: I mean the Fifth Symphony. "Roméo et Juliette, symphonie dramatique avec chœurs, solos de chant, et prologue en récitatif choral, op. 17," to give it its full title, was finished in 1838, produced in 1839 at the Conservatoire, and repeated three times within a short period. The work had a very mixed reception. Berlioz was never popular in Paris or among his own countrymen ; but all admitted that the general conception was colossal. It is now regarded as a classic throughout the world, but it is a big undertaking to produce. Little bits of it " would never please " as *entr'actes* or incidental music to a production of the play in London. The words are by Berlioz, inspired by Shakespeare, and versified by Emil Déschamps ; and the work is dedicated to Paganini, who a little earlier had presented Berlioz with twenty thousand francs to show his admiration for the earlier Symphonie Fantastique. Berlioz says in his autobiography : " I remember in one of my Campagna rides with Mendelssohn (this was during his tenure of the Prix de Rome) expressing my surprise that no one had ever written a scherzo on Shakespeare's sparkling little poem, *Queen Mab*. He, too, was surprised, and I was very sorry I had put the idea into his head. For years I lived in dread that he had used it : for he would have made it impossible, or at any rate very risky, for anyone to attempt to do it after him. Luckily he forgot." This was a very generous tribute to Mendelssohn's power as a fairy-music composer, coming from a musician in no very great sympathy with his style.

This symphony is scored for a very large orchestra. The first movement consists of a fine musical imitation of a street fight, culminating in the entrance of the Prince (on the full bass), who stops the fight. Then comes a choral prologue for contraltos and basses, giving a rough idea of the plot. Then a Queen Mab scene for tenor and chorus, and a great concert and ball given at the Capulets'. This finishes the second part. The third part is the love scene (Balcony scene as we call it) in Capulet's garden. There is some very exquisite love-music here ; and the whole movement, which is really the so-called " slow movement " of the conventional symphony, is very beautiful. The fourth section (Scherzo) is called " Queen Mab," and is one of those delicate, gossamer, fairylike works in which Berlioz so excels. Then come choral music for the funeral cortege of Juliet, and Romeo's invocation at the tomb of the Capulets. The finale takes place in the graveyard : Montagues and Capulets are both there, Friar Laurence explains everything, and there is reconciliation between the rival houses, ending in their swearing over the graves to be friends for ever. I know this is a very bald account. The work should be heard to be understood fairly ; but a very interesting couple of hours can be spent by a musician on the full score of this work in the British Museum reading-room. The text is given in both French and German. Wagner, in his letters from Paris, 1841, says of Berlioz : " He has no friend deemed worthy to be asked for counsel, none he would permit to draw his notice to this or that sin against form in his works. In regard to this, I was filled with regret by a hearing of his symphony, *Roméo et Juliette.* Amid the most brilliant inventions, this work is heaped with such a mass of trash and solecisms that I could not repress the wish that Berlioz had shown this composition before performance to some such man as Cherubini, who, without doing ·its originality the slightest harm, would certainly have had the wit to rid it of a quantity of disfigurements. . . . Wherefore Berlioz will always remain imperfect, and, maybe, shine as nothing but a transient marvel." There is some sound though exaggerated criticism in these sentences ; but Wagner could not have known on what sort of terms Cherubini and Berlioz were. That the latter could submit a work for correction to the former is impossible for anyone knowing anything about their personal and artistic relations to consider for a moment. Still, the personal criticism of one great composer by another is always interesting and informing.

Tschaikowsky's Overture-Fantaisie, *Roméo et Juliette,* is scored for an ordinary symphony orchestra with horn and harp. It is very modern and very emotional, and at times almost hysterical. The work begins in a quasi-organ manner, but the first subject is very bold. Whether it is to express Montague or Capulet I don't know. It seems too robust to express my idea of Romeo, but it may be Tschaikowsky's. The second subject is obviously Juliet, and the two themes are developed to the end, which, curiously enough, for the last few bars is quite lively. The work makes a very interesting contrast to Berlioz, but I suspect that the great Frenchman had a deeper insight into Shakespeare's poem than the Russian. Tschaikowsky's work could be done without any mention of Romeo and Juliet or Shakespeare; Berlioz's could not.

Joseph Joachim Raff, a composer whose name is unfortunately mostly associated with the well-known or notorious Cavatina, is a much underrated man. He was an indefatigable worker and an outstanding example of the fatuity of Carlyle's definition of genius. Undoubtedly Raff was no genius, but he was a composer of far from common ability. His four Shakespearian overtures, of which the one to *Romeo and Juliet* is the first, are all most interesting. They are not absolute programme music. They give the idea more than the story, but are none the worse for that. The *Romeo* overture opens with a fine broad theme for the horns, swiftly followed by a somewhat suave melody for the strings, the other instruments gradually joining in. The middle part is quite tragic, and the whole is carried out to a well-constructed finish. Without achieving great music, Raff rises to certain heights in this overture.

Hugo Pierson's concert overture *Romeo and Juliet*, op. 86, is very interesting, but not so much so as his symphonic poem *Macbeth*, which I described at some length in an earlier section. Composed for a large orchestra, it opens with a short *allegro appassionato* introduction; but this soon changes to a graceful theme typical of the luxurious life of Verona, broken in upon occasionally by suggestion of the hate between the rival houses of Montague and Capulet. This is followed by an amorous subject typical of Romeo, and by a gay theme for the great dance. The

Balcony scene is beautifully portrayed.   The remainder of
the music becomes high tragedy, and it remains so till the
very end.   The overture is quite short and not so difficult
as most of Pierson's work, and it is full of melody and
broad orchestral effects.   The themes are all original, as
is their treatment, and the tonality is interesting though
difficult to follow.

Edward German composed the whole of the music for
Forbes-Robertson's production of *Romeo and Juliet* at the
Lyceum, September 1895, and also dedicated it to him.
It is a complete piece of work, admirably carried out
and suited for the occasion.   It opens with a fine sombre
prelude, showing the atmosphere of hate which was
brooding over the otherwise pleasant town of Verona.
This feeling of hate and the love-music are the two most
important themes in the prelude, which finishes up with
six bars, *religioso*, to suggest the tomb.   For the remainder
of the music Mr German has himself made a selection of
themes containing all that is of the most importance.   The
curtain music for the first act is a broad theme in common
time, which serves to open the scene and is otherwise harmless.   Then comes the Peter *motif*—a good Old
English comedy theme with an excellent descending bass.
The March which follows is a thoroughly good Old English
march of the kind to which Mr German has accustomed us.
The Capulets' Reception music and Juliet's theme (I am
quoting Mr German) are graceful six-eight numbers, and
if taken a little faster than marked would make excellent
Old English country dances.   Even at the proper time
one expects to see shepherds, not great ladies and gentlemen.   The Love *motif* is sombre enough—Mr German
never seems to give his lovers time to be happy; but the
Nurse theme is a real bit of German at his best, and is
very welcome.   The music for Paris at the tomb of Juliet
is necessarily sad, and the Death theme, the last number,
is quite in keeping with the end of Shakespeare's tragedy.
There is a charming nocturne which makes a very effective

entr'acte, delicately scored and very original. The Pastoral, again, is a delightful composition. But the best number, to my mind, is the Pavane. Here Mr German has got the real Romeo-Juliet-Shakespeare atmosphere, and in this simple dance has done more to express in music what Shakespeare was showing to us than in his complicated prelude or in the rest of the incidental music. This Pavane is a real gem.

Joseph Holbrooke's poem for chorus and orchestra, *Queen Mab*, was first performed at the Leeds Festival in 1904. The chorus part is *ad lib.*, but if properly performed makes a very effective addition to the fairly large orchestra that Mr Holbrooke has scored for. The opening is in the guise of a scherzo, very brilliant and difficult ; then comes a long slow episode ; then much development ; and finally the entrance of the chorus. The time is *adagio*, and the words begin, " Arise, fair sun, and kill the envious moon," ending six lines afterwards. These lines are repeated again and again, quite in the so-called old-fashioned style ; the chorus dies away ; and the orchestra finishes the work with a coda *fortissimo*. Queen Mab has long since disappeared.

Johann Severin Svendsen, born 1840, Christiania, wrote a *Romeo and Juliet* overture, but there is no copy of it in the British Museum.

The following operas are mentioned in Mr Barclay Squire's interesting article on Shakespearian operas, from the book *Homage to Shakespeare*, 1916. As they more or less complete the list, I mention them ; but I cannot find copies of them or any reference as to their comparative merits, or otherwise :—Dramma per Musica, in 2 acts, pub. Berlin in 1773, with no composer's name ; opera by Benda, Gotha, 1776 ; T. G. Schwanenberg, Leipzig, 1776 ; L. Marescalchi, Rome, 1789 ; Von Rumling, Munich, 1790 ; Porta, Paris, 1806 ; Schuster, Vienna,

1809. This article gives a fairly complete list of the music inspired by our play. It seems curious that with so magnificent a theme only one composer—Berlioz, of course—should have risen to absolutely supreme heights. I suppose his work is performed very occasionally; whereas Gounod's is in every operatic repertory in the world.

THE TAMING OF THE SHREW

THIS play seems, on the whole, to have been very much avoided by musicians. There must be a certain amount of music in any work of Shakespeare, but producers appear to have been content to use old stuff and adapt it for this piece. **Noel Johnson** wrote some very pretty music for the Asche-Brayton production; but Sir Frank Benson's version had hardly any music in it: just a dance (the beautiful Rigadoon, by Rameau), a gavotte by Handel, and a song by Sir Henry Bishop, " Should he upbraid "— words not from the *Shrew*, nor even by Shakespeare.

A musical version, chiefly by **Braham** and **T. S. Cooke,** was produced in London in 1828. But the really important work on the subject is **Hermann Goetz's** opera, *Der Widerspenstigen Zähmung*, produced at Mannheim, 1874, book by Joseph Victor Erdmann. This work is Goetz's only complete opera, as, unfortunately for music, he died at the early age of thirty-five, in the height of his powers. His *Taming of the Shrew* is still in the repertory of the German opera-houses.

The characters have the same names as in the play—Katharina and Bianca, sopranos ; Hortensio and Lucentio, bass and tenor ; Baptista and Grumio, basses ; the Tailor, tenor ; and Petruchio, baritone.

The work begins with a full concert overture, a capital number, which would make an excellent opening for any production of the play. The themes are bold, striking, and original, though the composer shows throughout the strong influence of Schumann. The opera is in four acts, the first taking place in a street outside Baptista's house. Lucentio, with guitar, is singing a sentimental ballad, occasionally interrupted by Baptista's servants, who rush from the house singing " The Devil is loose in the house." Baptista asks them what is the matter, and the servants at once give notice on account of Katharina's outrageous behaviour. There is nothing much of Shakespeare in this act, but it makes a brilliant opening to the opera. Katharina then comes on the balcony and tells the people how good she is going to be. The neighbours all join in, and there is a beautiful bit of choral work for principals, neighbours, and chorus. All exit except Lucentio ; the chorus in the house sing an unaccompanied sort of evening hymn, the music dies away, the lights in Baptista's house go out, and Lucentio serenades Bianca.

Presently she appears on the balcony, and they sing a beautiful love duet, say good-night, and exit. Hortensio arrives to serenade her also, and quarrels with Lucentio, and the pair of them make such a noise that they waken poor old Baptista, who appears at the house door in his dressing-gown, with a light, still wondering if he will ever get any peace. Petruchio enters to a very blustering tune (the Petruchio *motif*, I call it). They make themselves known to each other, and Petruchio, in a beautiful and melodious song, describes his deeds in the past, just as in the play, and says what a poor opinion he has of the power of a woman's tongue. The act ends very happily, with Petruchio promising to woo and win Katharina.

The second act starts with a short prelude, *sostenuto* and slow, and as the curtain goes up Katharina and Bianca begin their quarrel scene, mostly on the former's part. Bianca produces a guitar and plays, while her sister says she will live and die a maid. Petruchio enters and woos the Shrew in a dramatic duet, and the act closes with a fine *ensemble* for the principals.

The third act opens, after hardly any orchestral introduction, with a quartet for Bianca, Lucentio, Hortensio, and Baptista, lamenting the absence of the bridegroom. Katharina joins in, very scornful about him, and the wedding guests enter, singing how difficult it is to have a wedding without a bridegroom. Then comes the familiar lesson scene. Lucentio sings the first lines of the first book of the *Æneid*, with his own additions. Hortensio also sings to his guitar—a method of music-teaching that even Bianca can see through ; and then Baptista enters, and, in a very lively number, gives the news of Petruchio's return. He arrives, more bluff and hearty than ever, clad in eccentric clothes, and hurries his bride-to-be to the church. The domestics of Baptista's house sing a chorus, showing how glad they are that Katharina is finally married and got rid of. The bridal party returns, and Petruchio announces his intention of departing at once. The close of the act must be very effective, according to the stage directions, when properly done. Grumio brings in two horses. Petruchio springs on one, Grumio rides off on the second, the chorus and principals singing lustily the while.

The fourth and last act opens with a male chorus, Petruchio's servants being bullied by Grumio, awaiting their master's return. The bridal pair make a fine entrance, and, as in the play, the husband finds fault with all the food, and sends it away. Katharina is left alone, and sings a beautiful and pathetic soliloquy on her difficult position. Grumio introduces the Tailor, and there is a very amusing quartet for the four. After this the action is much hurried. The changed Katharina arrives at her father's house ; her father congratulates his son-in-law on the admirable way in which he has reformed Katharina ; everyone is pleased, especially the servants of Baptista, and the whole work ends with a joyous *ensemble*, making a very brilliant close to the opera.

The opera was refused by innumerable managers, but was finally staged by Ernst Frank at Mannheim, 1874, where its success was immediate and decisive. The next year it was performed at Vienna, Leipsic, Berlin, and other

German towns, and it was also produced in London at a matinée at Drury Lane, October 12, 1878. In 1880 it was revived by the Carl Rosa Company at Her Majesty's, Minnie Hauk taking the part of Katharina. It very well deserves a revival at the present day. Every note of it would be fresh to nine hundred and ninety-nine opera-goers out of a thousand. All the parts are good, and ample scope is given for brilliant singing.

THE TEMPEST

OF all the plays *The Tempest* has been most popular with musicians. The earliest music to *The Tempest* is generally believed to be by **Robert Johnson,** who wrote settings of "Where the bee sucks" and "Full fathom five." The *Encyclopædia Britannica* is quite definite on the subject; but as Johnson was born in 1604, and Shakespeare died in 1616, and had left off writing plays for several years before his death, Johnson must, as I said in the Introduction, have been something of a musical prodigy.

The next in order seems to be **Matthew Locke's** instrumental music to an operatic version of *The Tempest* (based on Dryden-Davenant), played in London in 1673. This work was revived and revised with additional numbers by **Henry Purcell** in 1695. The exquisite "Come unto these yellow sands" was one of the additional numbers. In both of these adaptations the words are very much altered, or "improved," as the theatre people of the time thought; but a very good hotch-potch version can be made by taking the best numbers mentioned, scoring them lightly, and having them sung simply and not operatically.

Arne's "Where the bee sucks" is his best work, and, I think, the most beautiful of all the settings.

John Christopher Smith, Handel's pupil and amanuensis, composed two operas on *The Tempest*, one of which was produced in London in 1756. The overture is the usual

one of the period; but Ariel's storm song, which opens the
first act, beginning with a long orchestral prelude, is a very
original piece of work. It is a dramatic recitative with
elaborate orchestral accompaniment to the words, slightly
adapted, from Ariel's speech to Prospero in Act i., Scene 2.
The following numbers have no connection with Shakespeare's play, a delightful setting of " Come unto these
yellow sands," for Ariel, being the next Shakespearian lyric
taken—this for high soprano with strings, very florid but
melodious; and the music for " Full fathom five " is also
very much in keeping with the words. Caliban (baritone)
sings " No more dams I'll make for fish " to a rollicking
tune, and follows it with a curious song called " The owl
is abroad." The words are not by Shakespeare, but it
is said that it was a great favourite with audiences.

Ariel's song, " Before you can say come and go," is
very gracefully set, and has a charming *obbligato* part for
the violin; but Prospero's recitative, " Now doth my
project gather to a head," is Shakespeare's blank verse
set to music. The duet ends peacefully and happily with
a duet for Ferdinand and Miranda about " gentle love,
innocence, and chaste desire." On the whole the work is
disappointing. One could have done with a little more
Shakespeare and less of Christopher Smith's own librettist;
but it contains much charming music, some of which
would sound very fresh if revived now.

John Davy, a West-countryman, born at Exeter, 1763,
composed an overture and other music for *The Tempest*.
It is dedicated to the memory of John Philip Kemble, and
includes songs by Arne, Purcell, and Linley. The overture
is a very simple affair, bringing in Purcell's " Where the
bee sucks " and ",Come unto these yellow sands," and
is, therefore, not so independent of the rest of the music
as the overture of this period usually is.

After the overture comes **Linley's** graceful setting of
" O, bid your faithful Ariel fly," sung in Prospero's cave

by Ariel (the words by Dr Laurence). Then follows
a very simple so-called symphony by Davy, all very quiet
and peaceful, going into Linley's horrible " Storm Chorus."
Christopher Smith's Caliban song is introduced after the
" Storm "—" No more dams I'll make for fish," which
has a very cheerful tune; and Purcell's beautiful settings
of " Come unto these yellow sands " and " Full fathom
five " follow. Between Acts i. and ii. Davy introduced
a symphony by himself, consisting of a very simple Largo,
followed by an equally simple Rondo. The song and
chorus that follow are by Purcell, to words by Dryden,
beginning " King Fortune smiles," which, like the next
song by the same authors, are too interesting to pass over
in silence, though neither has any real connection with
Shakespeare. The music for the appearance of Fairies is
by Purcell, to words by Dryden, " Where does the black
fiend ambition reside ? ", and is for two bass voices and
chorus, with an interesting solo bassoon part.

The opening of the third act consists of a very pretty
symphony by Davy, in the form of an air with variations.
The only musical number in this act consists of a song,
very grotesque in style, for Caliban, words by Ben Jonson,
music by Christopher Smith. The prelude to the fourth
act is in march rhythm, a pleasant, cheerful piece of music,
composed by Davy. The setting of " Where the bee
sucks " is Arne's delightful one, and is sung by Ariel,
repeated by a quartet, with added words and the music
much elaborated, while, according to the stage directions,
Ariel and the spirits ascend into the sky. This is the last
number, but the untiring Linley has added an appendix
consisting of two songs for Ariel, " While you here do
snoring lie " and " Ere you can say come and go,"
and a duet for Juno and Ceres, entitled " Honour, riches,
marriage, blessing " ; all with words by Shakespeare from
this play—quite a concession on the part of a composer of
this period, especially of T. Linley himself.

Between R. Johnson's time and the present day I can

trace twenty operas on this subject, but none of them has held the stage. The only modern one that was produced in London seems to be **Halévy's** two-act opera *La Tempesta*, book by Scribe, produced at Her Majesty's in Italian. The story of how this work came to be composed is rather interesting. In October 1831, Mendelssohn gave a grand concert at Munich, and was so successful that he received a commission to compose an opera for the Munich theatre. He consulted with Immerman as to the libretto, and arranged with him for one founded on *The Tempest*. The composer and librettist, however, soon quarrelled, and the opera scheme lay dormant for some time. About the middle of October Mendelssohn was in communication with Lumley, lessee of Her Majesty's, for an opera, libretto by Scribe, on the same subject. Mendelssohn did not like this libretto, and finally turned it down; and Jacques François Fromental Elias, " a Jew whose real name was Levy," as Grove's *Dictionary* prettily phrases it, then set the libretto. Halévy was born in Paris, 1799, and studied at the Conservatoire under Cherubini. Having won the second prize twice, he finally carried off the Grand Prix de Rome itself.

The opera was produced at Her Majesty's, London, on June 14, 1850, and made an enormous success. The first act is opened by a chorus of Air Spirits, who obey the orders of Ariel. Sleeping Sylphs are wakened, and make together a most poetic choreographic effect, which is repeated again in the first tableau summoned by Prospero. Carlotta Grisi acted with great success as Ariel in this work, and Lablache was terrible and grotesque, though sometimes tender, as Caliban. Sontag was the Miranda, and the whole performance was conducted by our own Michael Balfe. The most popular numbers in the score were the cavatina, " Parmi una voce mormore "; the duet, " S' odio, orror di me non hai "; and the finale to the second act, which is full of movement and originality.

A lyrical drama, after Shakespeare, by Armand Silvestre

and Pierre Berton, music by **Victor Alphonse Duvernoy,** was produced in the Salle du Châtelet on November 24, 1880. This remarkable work won the Grand Prix for musical composition offered every two years by the town of Paris. It obtained a very well-deserved success at the first public performance for its great qualities of form and style. Much of the opera was greatly applauded, especially the duet of Ferdinand and Miranda, " Parle encore, que ta voix m'enivre," the dramatic trio, " Courbe-toi, vaincu sous la chaîne," the very original song of Caliban, the symphonic music descriptive of Miranda's sleep, the prelude to the third act, and the pretty ballet air of the Sylphs.

Larousse, the musical historian, says that it is a truly interesting work, and certainly produces a grand effect on the stage. The composer of this opera was born in Paris, 1842.

Zdenko Fibich's three-act opera, *Boûre*, or *Der Sturm* (1895), is a recent opera on this subject, and is by far the most modern in treatment. All Shakespeare's principal characters are present, and the libretto is very ingenious. There is no overture proper, but a fairly long orchestral introduction opens the first act ; it consists of very furious storm music, with Prospero's principal theme hammered out on the bass brass. As the curtain rises, Prospero and Miranda are discovered watching the storm ; the storm dies away, and Miranda, in a very melodious passage, asks her father all about it, and what has happened to the sailors and the ship which they have both seen in great difficulties. In a very dignified quasi-recitative passage Prospero tells her that the storm is of his own planning, and he then relates much of the story of his life and wrongs.

Though long, the orchestral accompaniment to this is so interesting and varied that no one could be bored by it. At the end Prospero puts Miranda to sleep, and after a beautiful orchestral interlude summons Ariel, who tells him in charming musical phrase what she has done with ship and sailors, and then exits to a delicate orchestral passage for wood wind. Prospero awakes Miranda, and sends her into his cave ; then he calls for Caliban, who presently appears to a grotesque tune played on the basses. To characteristic music he grumbles at his perpetual labour, till Prospero, angry, sends him off. Ariel and a spirit chorus now lure Alonzo and the rest, by their singing, to where Prospero is, and totally bewilder them ; a very beautiful *ensemble* follows for chorus and principals, which finishes on the exit of all except Prospero and Miranda. Ariel returns bringing Ferdinand, whom Miranda recognises as the being she had seen in her dream. Ariel sings a very pretty adaptation of " Full fathom five," and the two lovers-to-be make friends, Prospero looking on unseen. Suddenly Prospero breaks in upon them very angrily, and displays to Ferdinand some of his miraculous powers, causing lightning and thunder, and finally paralysing him.

This is all done to a most effective and appropriate setting, and the curtain falls on the first act to a fine dramatic situation, much heightened by excellent music.

The second act opens with a fairly long orchestral prelude ; it is on a dominant pedal, fifty-five bars in length, and depicts the depths of a tropical forest. Ferdinand sings, and is presently joined by Miranda. Now we have a really amusing comedy scene for Trinculo, Stephano, and Caliban, the last-named having an excellent grotesque song, in which the others join. The drinking scene is very well set to music, the part of Caliban being strongly marked and individual.

Ariel breaks in on this festive scene with her spirit chorus, and the comedians exit. Gonzalo and the other nobles enter, and, as in the play, spirits bring mysterious food and drink, and strange music is everywhere heard. All this is capitally done. Ariel, in a dramatic manner, denounces them all as " men of sin." Prospero then enters, to a fine *maestoso* bass movement, explaining everything ; and the act finishes with a solemn march, to which all the spirits of Earth, Air, Fire, and Water enter and do homage to Prospero.

The last act opens with a long prelude signifying Prospero's magic powers. Sometimes we get charming light Ariel music, sometimes music suggesting a deeper, more awful, kind of magic, and sometimes a grotesquely comic dance rhythm, which is, nevertheless, almost sad, suggesting poor Caliban. It is altogether a most interesting prelude, and would make an excellent concert number by itself. The curtain rises on Prospero's cave to mysterious sounds; alchemical instruments are scattered about, and great books in ancient bindings lie on the table. Prospero and Ariel are discovered. The Spirit tells him that Caliban and his friends are going to kill him in his sleep. Ferdinand and Miranda enter hand in hand, and Prospero summons the Spirits, who sing sweetly to the lovers. Presently Caliban and his friends enter, and Ariel and the other spirits chase them away jeeringly. Ariel claims liberty ; and, to sonorous music, Prospero renounces his magic arts. With a great musical noise his cave disappears, and the scene changes to the landscape of the first act. In the rocky cove Alonzo's ship is ready to sail ; Prospero calls on Ariel for the last time ; and, to solemn tones, all the mortals enter from different parts of the stage. The end is now very near. Ariel is set free ; Prospero promises all a comfortable, safe voyage ; the sailors sing of the joys of home life ; and the curtain falls to the Spirits singing of their new freedom. The Caliban and Spirit music is the best part of the opera. All the mysterious magical effects are most impressively done, but the composer is not so happy with his lovers. The orchestral interludes are excellent, and the many choruses of unseen Spirits are most melodious, and not too difficult.

Alfred M. Hale, a very progressive young composer, has written an opera on this subject, parts of which were performed at the Queen's Hall on February 28, 1912. Among the numbers given was a duet for Miranda and Ferdinand. A well-known musical critic writes as follows concerning this number : " Mr Hale has written vocal parts in the style of an intoned conversation; no really vocal phrases are apparent, but the text is moaned to a vague backing of orchestral activity. Occasionally one heard snatches of *Tristan* or *Pelléas*. All is vast, vague, and vacuous. Mr Hale's orchestra breathes with its mouth wide open." So we will leave it at that.

Sullivan's *Tempest* contains some of his finest music. Composed at Leipsic when he was Mendelssohn Scholar, it has all the freshness of youth and none of its immaturity. It was first performed at the Crystal Palace, June 8, 1862, and was enthusiastically received, Charles Dickens complimenting the young composer very highly. Though not written expressly for the theatre, the music can be used almost as it stands; but I have never heard it without additional numbers. When it was adopted for Henrietta Hodson's production, Sullivan's " Where the bee sucks " was cut out and Arne's substituted. Arne's setting is his best work, and, in my opinion, the most beautiful of all the versions extant ; but Sullivan's is fine too, and the former did not blend with the rest of the score but stood out and spoilt the whole musical scheme.

Taubert wrote capital incidental music for this play, but I have never heard it without additional numbers. Sir Frank Benson used a great deal of this setting in his production of *The Tempest*, but he made use of much other music as well. In his version the play began with a " Storm Chorus " by Haydn, supposed to have been inspired by his first (a bad) crossing to England ; at least, this was the tradition in the Benson company. Then he went on to Taubert for " Come unto these yellow sands" and " Full fathom five," both very pretty arrangements for Ariel (soprano) and chorus ; back to Arne for " Where the bee sucks," and to Sullivan for " Honour, riches." A song for Ariel, " Oh, bid thy faithful Ariel fly," by T. Linley, was interpolated, the words not even by Shakespeare. For the closing scenes, Sir Frank returned to

Taubert; and if the whole affair was a hotchpotch, it was a very agreeable one.

The last, and quite the most important, music written for *The Tempest* since Sullivan's time is Humperdinck's. **Engelbert Humperdinck** is well known in England as the composer of the opera *Hänsel und Gretel*, the scores of *Königskinder* and *The Miracle*, but few English people know his Shakespearian works. His music to *The Tempest* was first heard at a great production of the play in Berlin at the Neue Schauspielhaus on October 25, 1906. It consists of a long prelude, running into storm melodrama music for the whole of the first scene, calming down beautifully for Miranda's first entrance. All the lyrics and choruses are set, and in all there are eighteen important numbers. The music is difficult, and the chorus and orchestra must be on a large scale; but it would make a very interesting production if it could be done exactly as the composer devised it, with no added numbers, extra lyrics, or pseudo-Elizabethan bilge. Here are ninety pages of closely printed pianoforte score; enough, surely, for the most old-fashioned producer without additional numbers. Very effective use is made of the male and female chorus, singing *bouche fermée* instead of the orchestra playing, as melodrama music. Ariel's " Where the bee sucks " is a charming setting, and the choruses and dances are most carefully and reverentially done. There is no German equivalent to Shadwell, Davenant, or Dryden. Here we have nothing but the exact text of Shakespeare, and really it seems quite enough. The Prospero *motif*, a fanfare, occurring frequently, holds the entire work together, and the magic music would be a great help to any Shakespeare production. I hope one day to see a straight production of this play with the music as composed.

Berlioz was early attracted to *The Tempest*, and even called one of the ladies he adored—Miss Moke, subsequently

Mme. Pleyel—Ariel. At the end of 1828, after the failure at rehearsal of the Symphonie Fantastique, he was asked to write something for Girard, conductor of the Théâtre Italien. He then composed his Fantasia with choruses on *The Tempest*, but Girard at once saw it was too big for his theatre and could only be done at the Opéra. There was to be a concert for the Artists' Benevolent Fund, and the work was accepted for performance by the director of the Academy, M. Loubbert, of whose care and kindness during the production Berlioz speaks most highly. He quotes Shakespeare about him (he often quoted Shakespeare), saying to a friend, " He was a man, Horatio." I cannot do better than transcribe the composer's interesting account of the first performance, taken from his *Autobiography* : " All went splendidly at rehearsal ; everything seemed to smile, when, with my usual luck, an hour before the concert, there broke over Paris the worst storm that had been known for fifty years. The streets were flooded, practically impassable, and for the first half of the concert when my *Tempest*, damned *Tempest*, was being played, there were not more than three hundred people in the place." Just Berlioz's luck ! Something nearly always went wrong with his work in Paris. In London, Petrograd, Berlin, anywhere else, he was immensely successful, but in Paris never quite a success, even at the height of his fame. The second performance, the following year, was much less unfortunate. Of the work itself Berlioz writes : " It is new, fresh, grand, sweet, tender, surprising."

It is a pity composers do not tell us more often what they think of their own works. I mean in autobiographies and signed articles, of course ; not, as has sometimes happened, in inspired articles written by their friends, or in anonymous ones written by themselves.

To come to the work itself, Berlioz incorporated it in his *Lelio, or The Return to Life* (lyric melodrama). This is one of the most extraordinary hotchpotches in all music. It begins with a ballad by Goethe, then there is a long postrophe to Shakespeare, then a brigand's song and chorus, then a song of bliss ; finally, the composer, Lelio or Berlioz, decides to write a fantasia on *The Tempest*, and calls on Shakespeare to stand by him. The orchestra and chorus then perform the fantasia. It is scored for full orchestra, but also for two pianos *à quatre mains*. The first number is a chorus of air spirits, soprani, alti, and tenori —1 and 2 calling on Miranda to come to her destined husband. (This is a rough translation.) After this comes a long orchestral interlude with a great *crescendo* and *diminuendo*, returning again to the Miranda chorus. The next is also a long orchestral interlude, introducing Caliban. The chorus shout *fortissimo* at him, calling him "Orrido monstro," which, I believe, means "horrid monster." After another long orchestral bit, the chorus again begins about Miranda, and sings a farewell chant to her as she is leaving the island. The coda is marked *più animato con fuoco*, and keeps up *animato* to the end. Whether it is supposed to show general relief on the part of the inhabitants of the island on the departure of Prospero and the rest of the mortals, or sorrow for the same reason, I do not profess to know. Lelio (Berlioz) says a few words to the performers, finishing, " You have indeed made progress, so much so that we may henceforth attempt works of greater depth than this feeble sketch." But this " feeble sketch " makes a very difficult work to tackle ; and if Berlioz had developed it, Heaven only knows where we should end !

La Tempête, Fantaisie pour orchestre by **P. Tschaikowsky,** is a very long and complicated symphonic poem, with a definite programme. It really tells a good deal of the story of Shakespeare's play-poem. It opens with " The Sea." After a few preliminary bars for wind, the strings *pianissimo,* and very much divided, play without any change of expression for fifty-three bars, and for the same number of bars the bass is F, with occasional changes to F sharp. It is a wonderful tone picture of a calm sea. Then comes Ariel, very light and feathery, presently ordered to bring about a great storm ; and it comes—quite one of the most terrific in all music. The storm having calmed down, we get the love-music of Ferdinand and Miranda—very timid music, but finally swelling up to a fine *forte* effect ; however, before this happens there is an amusing dialogue (if one may use the word) between Ariel and Caliban. To most impressive music, Prospero surrenders his magic powers, and the mortals quit the island. The sea music starts again just as in the opening, and the work ends on a perfectly calm sea even as it began. It is, of course, as with all the composer's greater works, very difficult, and scored for a large orchestra; but its effects are certain, and it is grateful to conduct or play. The storm is undoubtedly one of the most graphic imitations of Nature in all musical art.

Frederick Corder's Concert Overture " Prospero " is a very good example of the composer's work. It was produced in 1885, and the *motto* is from *The Tempest*, Act iii., Scene 3 : " What harmony is this ? My good friends, hark ! "

It opens with a *forte* theme for trombones and tuba, obviously Prospero himself; followed by flute solo, again obviously Ariel, accompanied by *pianissimo* violin (very high sustained chords) and harp. These two subjects hold a sort of dialogue in which Prospero has the last word till the *Allegro con fuoco* commences.

This theme is a very high, swift, semiquaver passage for violins, with some occasional help from the wood wind. It leads to a subject for 'cello of quite a melodic, easy-going character, which might easily be Ferdinand, and, as the first violins join in, Miranda. Then enters Prospero with his trombones against this sweetness, and the drama of the overture begins—Prospero drowns his books, Ariel is heard singing joyfully, but somewhat sadly, and, in the end, the spirits of the island, free at last, are heard in a great rejoicing.

I wish Mr Corder had written even the vaguest programme for this overture. I have tried to write one, but I may be wrong the whole time ; anyway, I have done my best, and

10

can heartily express my great admiration for the overture and the attitude it takes according to my reading of the play.

Mr Corder has also set " Come unto these yellow sands " and " Full fathom five " for soprano and female chorus, with harps for the first number, and contralto and orchestra for the second ; both are melodious and effective, though there is much repetition of the words.

J. F. Duggan, born 1847, died 1894, whose name does not appear in any musical biographical dictionary that I can find, has done a couple of interesting settings of songs for Caliban. The first, curiously enough, is for a tenor : I have often thought of Caliban musically, but never as a tenor ; still, here it is. The words begin, " No more dams I'll make for fish," and the setting is quite appropriately grotesque. The second is elaborate. It was first sung by Sir Charles Santley, to whom it was dedicated, and is for high baritone. The words begin, " Art thou afeared ? " and the music is quite decorative in its harmonic progressions, and gives points quite excellently to the curious lines in which Caliban describes the musical wonders of the island to Trinculo and Stephano, while Ariel plays on his tabor and pipe. This song was published in 1871, and that is the only further biographical detail I can give.

Clarence Lucas, a Canadian composer (b. 1866), has written a very brilliant Scherzo for piano solo, entitled " Ariel." He has taken as his motto Shakespeare's words, " On the bat's back I do fly," and has certainly illustrated the familiar passage with great dexterity. It is a gossamer piece of work, and, though difficult, is highly effective. It bears strong traces of the composer's years of study at the Paris Conservatoire.

Joseph Spaight, a clever young English composer, has written a string quartet called " Ariel," which is really very interesting. The work is divided into eight sections, each one expressing some Ariel episode in the play. The episodes are described in a few words, such as " On a ship in a storm," " Invisible," " Playing time on tabor and pipe and leading Caliban, Stephano, and Trinculo away." They are highly descriptive, but one may well question whether the string quartet is the proper vehicle for such programme music.

TIMON OF ATHENS

THE only opera mentioned by Mr Barclay Squire that might have been founded on this play is *Timone, Misantropo*, by the **Emperor Leopold I.,** produced at Vienna in 1696. Leopold I., Emperor of the West, was born in 1640, and educated by the Jesuits for the Church, and he probably learned music from them. I have read fine biographies of him ; but though I find he was not a really good ruler, there is no mention of his gifts as a musician. It would be interesting to discover a copy of an opera, libretto by the King of Dramatists, music by the Emperor of the West, King of Hungary and Bohemia ; but with the exception of the name and the date I can discover no record of the work at all : not even a popular selection for the pianoforte —Leopold-Liszt !

In 1678, Thomas Shadwell produced his version of *Timon of Athens*, under the title " The History of Timon of Athens, the Man Hater, made into a play by Thomas Shadwell." Of the atrocities committed by the adapter on Shakespeare in this version it is not easy to speak with restraint. Suffice it to say that ten years after the production Shadwell became Poet Laureate ! The masque in Act i. is written entirely by Shadwell, with music by **Henry Purcell.** Whether this work comes legitimately within the scope of my theme I am not certain. Undoubtedly the author and composer must have been under the influence of, if not inspired by, Shakespeare : as we have so little music for this strange play, I will therefore make a short analysis of the masque. Julian Marshall, in his foreword to the Purcell

Society's edition, says : " This work was not well calculated to inspire the genius of Purcell. Written to order, and perhaps in some haste, the score is slight in character and design." There are several beautiful numbers.

The work consists of an overture and thirteen numbers. The first part of the overture is taken from the " Trumpet Sonata," and is fairly familiar to lovers of Purcell. The duet for two nymphs that follows is preceded by a " Symphonie of Pipes " to imitate birds : this is played on two flutes with a very pretty effect. The bass song, " Return, revolting rebels," sung by Bacchus, has a fine bold melody ; and a slow trio in the minor is in strong contrast to the principal theme. The best chorus is " Who can resist such mighty charms ? ", which, though simple in construction, has some fine broad effects.

The last duet and chorus, for Cupid and Bacchus, is very bright and melodious, composed in six-four time, and makes a merry end to the masque. After the epilogue comes a " Curtain tune on a ground," for strings only—by far the most interesting number in the piece. The persistent use of the idiom of " false relation " throughout the whole piece gives it a curious interest ; and the contrapuntal and harmonic devices are also quite elaborate. I should think there is more of the real Timon in this one number than in all Shadwell's perversions.

TWELFTH NIGHT

In spite of its great poetical beauties, *Twelfth Night* has not attracted many composers. There is only one opera that I can trace, and that is *Cesario*, by **K. G. Wilhelm Taubert,** produced in Berlin at the Royal Opera House in 1874. There is no attempt to foster the delusion that anyone who is not next door to an idiot could ever mistake Sebastian for Viola, or *vice versâ*. Viola, in this version, is a soprano, and her brother a tenor-baritone, so it is hard to understand how even Orsino was taken in ; but he was (and he a baritone, not a tenor !).

The opera opens with an overture, conventional and not very characteristic, and the curtain rises on a scene in Illyria, near Orsino's palace.

A chorus of maidens, wives, sailors, children, and musicians is discovered, singing a very bright and melodious number, which, though very tuneful, does not help the action at all. The second scene opens with storm music bringing on Viola and the Sea Captain.

The librettist, Emil Taubert, does not adhere any too closely to the original, so I will just describe the most effective numbers. Sir Toby's drinking song in the first act is a thoroughly good German drinking song, with the usual low bass E for the end ; and directly afterwards Sir Andrew has a grotesque love-song with no little humour in it.

In the fourth scene there is a very sentimental duet between Viola and Orsino. As the work progresses we get farther and farther away from Shakespeare, and so I leave the only opera founded on this exquisite play. I think a great deal of its weakness is due to the librettist cutting out Feste, the clown. There is no " Come away, Death," " O mistress mine," or " When that I was."

So it is with pleasure that I turn to **Humperdinck's** delightful music for Reinhardt's production at the Deutsches Theater, Berlin, produced on October 17, 1907. The first scene is in Orsino's court (as in Shakespeare), and gives the whole romantic atmosphere of the rest of the play. Most producers begin with the short scene of Viola's shipwreck, thus cunningly avoiding the whole idea of the plot. Two violins, viola, and viol-da-gamba are discovered playing the music of " O mistress mine " on the stage; and if it is impossible to obtain a viol-da-gamba, the composer allows one to use a violoncello. Also there is a guitar off the stage. The text is closely followed. The setting ('cello solo) for the words " If music be the food of love " is very beautiful; and until the Duke's words, " Enough, no more," the incidental music fits in with every shade of expression in that perfect monologue. The next number is the serenade for the clown (Feste). He is supposed to accompany himself on the guitar, but the guitar part is cued in for the harp if the singing-actor has not enough skill on the instrument. It is a very charming song, not in the least like the settings of the same words to which we are all so accustomed, but none the worse for that. The catch " Hold thy peace " is a perfect canon at the unison, sung by Sir Toby, Sir Andrew, and the clown. All the verses in the kitchen scene are set to music, the versatile clown playing the accompaniments on his ever-ready guitar.

In Act ii., Scene 4, no expensive prima-donna is called upon to sing " Come away, Death." Orsino simply sends for Feste, and tells his orchestra to play the tune while they are all waiting.

When the clown does arrive to sing the song the audience has been played into the exact mood Shakespeare wanted; and the number, lovely as it is, gets a better chance of success than if the orchestra had been playing something quite different (as I have often heard), or an entirely new character, a singing woman, had been introduced for this special number. Feste sings " Hey, Robin, jolly Robin " and " I am gone, sir," to specially composed music still accompanied by the guitar, and there are two settings by Humperdinck of the epilogue song, " When that I was." Both are written for Feste; but the first one is accompanied only by the guitar, while the second has an elaborate orchestral accompaniment. You can take your choice; both settings are equally good.

This music, both in form and expression, is, perhaps, the ideal music for a Shakespearian production. Nothing is forced on the hearer. When Shakespeare wanted music he said so, either in his stage directions or in the text. This is exactly what Humperdinck has given us. Never to my knowledge has Shakespeare's text been so reverently treated by any composer or producer. I often think that it is not entirely the fault of the composer of Shakespearian music that so much of it is superfluous; perhaps a little blame may lie with the actor-manager-producer, who must have a march to bring him on and take him off at every entrance or exit.

Sir Alexander Mackenzie's delightful *Twelfth Night* overture was first produced at a Richter concert in 1888. Though it is not exactly programme music, Sir Alexander gives occasional quotations on the score indicating his intentions.

The opening is labelled Act ii., Scene 5, Malvolio (taking up letter), " By my life, this is my lady's hand." The 'cellos, basses, and violas play a unison quaver passage of introduction, and Malvolio obviously speaks through the medium of a bassoon. The clarinets and the rest of the wood wind join in, the strings sustaining an accompaniment; and so the first episode finishes.

The next is labelled Act ii., Scene 5, Sir Toby, " Why, thou hast put him in such a dream that when the image of it leaves him he must run mad." Then comes, to my idea, the triumphal music of Malvolio. This is quickly followed by a label, Act ii., Scene 3, Sir Toby, " Shall we rouse the night owl in a catch ? " and for a few moments we have bright sounds of revelry ; but very swiftly the music gets slow and *piano*, and presently we return to Act i., and the words on the score are, " O, she that hath a heart of that frame, To pay this debt but to a brother," etc. This subject is very beautiful, and admirably portrays Orsino's love for Cesario. After this comes a bright, melodious episode working up to a *fortissimo* climax. Then we have another label, Act iv., Scene 2, Malvolio, " Fool, there never was a man so notoriously abused. I am as well in my wits as thou art."

The music then proceeds in *fugato* manner for a long time, and there are no more directions or quotations from the text in the score till towards the end. This is now the regular coda, and very brilliant it is. But just before the close one finds the label, Act v., Scene 1, Malvolio, " I'll be revenged on the whole pack of you " ; the original Malvolio *motif* being played by the violas and 'cellos and taken up by the rest of the orchestra. The whole finishes *fortissimo* and very cheerfully. There is a curious kettledrum solo in the third bar before the end. Taken all round, this overture is quite one of the best Shakespearian commentaries extant. Without being in the least pedantic, it has a smack of the period ; and as a sheer, joyous bit of comedy it ranks very high in the repertory of Shakespearian music.

Sir Henry Bishop's third pasticcio opera was founded on *Twelfth Night*. It was produced at the Royal, Drury Lane, in 1820. Contrary to his usual custom there is no overture, and the first number is a song for viola with bassoon *obbligato* to the words, " Full many a glorious morning " from the 33rd Sonnet. The first half is very unlike the composer's usual manner, but in the second he soon gets back to his original style. The next number is a quintet with words from *The Two Gentlemen*

of Verona—" Who is Sylvia ? "   The melody of the first
verse is by Ravenscroft (1714), that of the second by
Morley (1595), and the whole is arranged by Sir Henry ;
so there is not much unity of style about it, though if
well sung and unaccompanied it should be effective.   The
duet " Orpheus with his lute," words by Fletcher, for Viola
and Olivia, is really too bad ; and with pleasure we turn
to a quartet by Thomas Ford (1580) and D. Calcott (1766).
It is called " Come o'er the brook, Bessé, to me."   The
first line is from *King Lear*, Act ii., Scene 6, but in the
text it is " bourne " not " brook."   The rest of the lines
are spurious.   The first verse is by Ford, the second by
Calcott, and the whole arranged by Bishop ; but this time
he has thrown in a harmonica part, the first that I have
met with in this orchestration.   The quartet and chorus
at the end of the second act are by Bishop; the words,
some of them from the second part of *Henry IV.*, and
some spurious.   The whole finale is very pretentious and
of no real musical value.   In Act iii. we have the inevitable cavatina, " Take all my loves," from the Sonnet
No. 40, sung by Olivia.   It is a most sugary song ; only a
few lines are taken, and repeated *ad nauseam*.   The duet
Olivia and Viola, called " Cesario," is adapted by Bishop
from a work I cannot trace (by a certain Winter).   The
only composer of that name in any musical biography is
Peter von Winter, born at Mannheim in 1755, and pupil of
Browning's celebrated Abt Vogler.   The words are a very
corrupt version of Olivia's speech in Act iii., Scene 1 of
this very play, and the music sometimes fits in and sometimes does not.

Kit Marlowe's " Crabbed age and youth," set by Bishop
for Olivia, has a fine cadenza duet with the flute, but is
otherwise not notable ; and " Bid me discourse," which
follows, is too well known to need mention.   An old setting
of the Clown's song, " When that I was," is arranged by
Bishop for the finale.   Viola and Olivia have one chorus
to themselves, very *rubato*.   The melody and chorus are
frequently changed, rhythmically and melodically, but it

makes a good finish to a very extraordinary mix-up of styles and composers. True to his ideals, Bishop does not use " Come away, Death," or " O mistress mine," two of the loveliest lyrics in the language—I suppose because they happen to occur in *Twelfth Night* !

During his second visit to London, **Haydn** composed his single contribution to Shakespearian song. It is contained in the set of six " Original Canzonets, composed for an English Lady of Position." The words are from *Twelfth Night*, beginning " She never told her love," and the song is very pathetic. Curiously enough for the period, the words " Smiling at grief " are the only ones repeated. The canzonet opens with a long symphony for piano. The voice part is melodious and vocal ; the harmonies are more complicated than is usual with Haydn, and there is more liberal use made of the chord of the diminished seventh than one looks for in his work. The voice part is of just an octave's range, and there are no aggressive *coloratura* passages or high notes.

The only work of **Johannes Brahms** in which I can trace the direct inspiration of Shakespeare is his setting of the Clown's song, " Come away, Death," from *Twelfth Night*, for trio of female voices, harp, and two horns. This is an exquisite little work, very complete ; there is hardly any repetition of the words : just at the end Brahms repeats " to weep there," but that is all. The combination of female voices, harp, and horns seems on paper to be rather eccentric, but in practice it is admirable, used as skilfully as Brahms has used it. This trio was not written for the play. In any decent production the song must be given to Feste, but how often is it ? Time after time I have seen a strange woman in tights dragged on to sing one of the numerous Wardour Street versions, and no one seems to mind. Without this song, the whole character of Feste, one of the best of all the Shakespearian clowns, sinks into almost nothingness.

Perhaps somewhere, hidden away in some old music catalogue, I may find something more of Brahms in relation to Shakespeare. Indeed, I hope so. What a Hamlet overture he could have written !

The bridal song, " Roses, their sharp spines being gone," and graceful dance (Malvolio), composed for Sir Herbert Tree's revival of *Twelfth Night*, make one wish that the composer, **Paul Rubens**, had devoted more time to this kind of work. The words, by Fletcher, are beautifully set ; and though there is no attempt at intentional archaism, there is an inimitable quaintness about this song, and the graceful dance which always accompanies Malvolio's entrances and exits, that is hard to find in modern Shakespearian music.

Augustus Barratt's setting of " Come away, Death," in the same production, is very beautiful. **Frederick Corder's** version of the same lyric for a trio of female voices and piano is a sad little number ; but I wish he would set the words straight, without repetitions.

Sir Charles Villiers Stanford's settings of the " Clown's songs " in *Twelfth Night* were not written for any special production, and were first sung by Mr Plunket Greene. There is no needless repetition of the words, every syllable being given its exact musical value ; so, from several points of view these versions are nearly perfect. The first, " O mistress mine," has a flowing though not very significant melody, and a graceful accompaniment. The second, " Come away, Death," is naturally of a very sombre nature, the harmonies being rather more elaborate than in the other two songs. The last lyric, " The rain it raineth every day," is, to my mind, much the best of the three. It is a very merry song, and the major effect and the little florid voice passage at the end make a charming close. Unfortunately, Sir Charles omits the last verse but one.

Dr Arne's setting is beautiful. It has a curious burden to it, in the accompaniment only ; but the words are sadly chopped about.

Sullivan's " O mistress mine " is quite one of his most effective songs ; and there is a beautiful flowing *obbligato* in the accompaniment which suggests that Sir Andrew, who played on the " viol-de-gamboys," was playing it for the Clown.

J. L. Hatton's setting of " When that I was " is quite pretty, but he plays the deuce with the words. The exquisitely quaint first line, " When that I was and a little tiny boy " becomes " When I was a tiny boy "; the last verse but one is entirely omitted; and the last verse of all is quite spoilt. There can be no possible excuse for Hatton or anyone else changing " But that's all one ; our play is done, and we'll strive to please you every day," into " But that's all one, our song is done, for the rain it raineth every day." This song, for tenor solo and four-part male chorus, won a prize given by the Melodists' Club. I suppose it was a word-distorting contest, and I congratulate the judges on a fine decision.

Samuel Coleridge Taylor's setting of " O mistress mine " is interesting in several ways. It is not in the least like any other musical version of the same words, and, though they are set quite straightforwardly, the general effect is curiously bizarre. The accompaniment is in the style of a guitar serenade, which is, of course, thoroughly in keeping with the stage situation, although the song itself was not composed for any special stage performance.

THE TWO GENTLEMEN OF VERONA

WITH the exception of the perfect lyric " Who is Sylvia ? " composers have left this play severely alone ; but **Sir Henry Bishop** certainly produced a pasticcio opera on *The Two Gentlemen of Verona* at the Royal, Covent Garden, in 1821. The work is the usual jumble of words from the plays, poems, and sonnets, set to music for the most part by Bishop. There is an overture which is really a string of tunes, mostly in C major, not labelled by the composer, and which do not occur later in the opera. It is a very bad example of a very bad class of so-called overture. The first song is a setting of the fifth to the twelfth lines of the Sonnet No. 64, sung by a character called Philippo, who does not appear in Shakespeare's play. It was performed by a Master Longhurst, a boy of some importance in his time, as he is mentioned by name in several books of reference regarding this song. The song in question is not worth very much, but is a good example of how a perfect sonnet may be transformed into a very indifferent song. This is followed by a duet for Philippo and Julia, with words from Shakespeare's 92nd Sonnet, but the first line is unhappily changed from " But do thy worst to steal thyself away," into " Save, though you strive to steal yourself away." The improvement is obvious ! and the musical setting quite in keeping with the improvement in the text ; only a few lines of the poem are sung, but oh ! how often repeated !

Sylvia has a great show in the next number. It is an extraordinary perversion of the Sonnet No. 109, " Oh, never say that I was false of heart," a poem that any decent-

minded pirate or burglar would have left alone. Still, Sir
Henry rushes in with what is officially described as a
bravura song. Certainly only lines 1–4 and 13–14 are set
to music, but how the few words are contorted! In the
coda Sylvia sings on the word " all," fourteen bars first
and then fifteen!

A society for the protection of sonnets should certainly
be formed. The ever-useful *Passionate Pilgrim* is used
for a mixture of Dr Arne and Bishop as an unaccompanied
quartet, " Good night, good rest," and we will leave it
at that; but the following number cannot be lightly treated.
It is difficult to forgive a composer who seizes on *the* perfect sonnet in the world and writes a "Solo Brilliante" on
the first four lines. These are certainly correctly printed,
save that the word " curse " (Shakespeare) is transformed
into " moan " (Bishop), and lines 9–12, with endless repetitions, are dragged in for the second half. This solo ends
with a long cadenza for voice and flute, the voice only using
the first half of the word " heaven "; there are just thirty
bars on the syllable " hea-"! The four-part round, " To
see his face," words from *Venus and Adonis* (only the first
four lines of stanza 183 are set), is an ingenious and entertaining piece of work, and should be most effective. For
some strange reason, " Who is Sylvia? " is set as a quintet,
with Julia on the top line. The first half of the melody is
by Bishop, but the second half is believed to be by Rousseau;
anyhow, no one would quarrel now as to how to apportion
the requisite blame; the " dishonours " appear to be
equally divided, except that Rousseau, being a Swiss,
could not be expected to show so tender a regard for
Shakespeare as Shakespeare's own fellow-countryman
Bishop did. The cavatina sung by Julia is to the first
eight lines of the 73rd Sonnet; and the male chorus,
" Now the hungry lion roars," is, of course, from one of
Puck's speeches in *A Midsummer Night's Dream*, but is
sadly cut and altered.

The duet, " On a Day," words from *Love's Labour's Lost*,
and also *The Passionate Pilgrim*, is another " I know a

bank "-like thing, and quite as uninteresting.   Julia's next song, " Should he upbraid," is familiar to all, and the words are founded on a speech of Baptista in *The Taming of the Shrew*.   The finale is a duet by Sylvia and Julia, assisted by the full chorus : its title is " How like a winter," and the words are partly adapted, very freely, from the first four lines of the 97th Sonnet, and from the masque in *As You Like It.*

A stranger jumble of words could hardly be conceived; yet this opera was quite successful, and no one seemed to think any the worse of Bishop, who was mainly responsible for its monstrosities.

Dr Arne's version of " Who is Sylvia ? " is really a very charming song, very melodious, very vocal, and full of delicate grace-notes.   The last verse is set as a trio, but can be sung as a solo without spoiling the composer's intentions ;   in   fact,   he   says   it   may   be   done   without additional voices.

Macfarren's part-song is very good—I mean Sir George's, not Walter's.   Both have set the words.   But the best setting of " Who is Sylvia ? " must for ever remain **Schubert's**—one of the perfect songs of the world.

THE WINTER'S TALE

THERE is only one opera, *Hermione*, by **Max Bruch,** founded on *The Winter's Tale*, and very little other music has been inspired by it, though the story possesses great operatic possibilities.

Engelbert Humperdinck's music for the Reinhardt production in Berlin, September 15, 1906, is, as usual with his incidental music, perfectly appropriate—not a superfluous note in it ; and also as usual in these productions, Shakespeare's Act i., Scene 1, is Reinhardt's. Before the rise of the curtain an orchestra of wood wind, horns, and harp plays soft and solemn music (called " Tafelmusik " in the score) behind the scenes, and the orchestra continues till a fanfare of trumpets announces the entrance of Leontes, Hermione, and their suite.

There is no more music until we come to Act iii., Scene 2, when, to open the Court of Justice scene, we have a broad, dignified fanfare, *quasi marcia*, scored for trombones, tuba, and drums, and part of this is played at the end of the scene. This is the motive associated with the Oracle.

At the end of Act iii., Scene 3, Time, a chorus, enters, and solemn music plays during his speech, composed in the manner of the Oracle. In the meantime, an act-change has been made, and without pause the curtain rises on the fourth act ; the music dying away as Polixenes and Camillo speak, swelling up on their exit and running into the symphony of Autolycus's song, " When daffodils begin to peer." This is very beautifully set, and the composer adds the verse from the end of the scene, which makes six verses instead of five ; but this is quite legitimate, as the last verse is obviously part of the whole lyric, though separated from the rest by some dialogue.

The music to open the fourth scene is called " Sunday Bells." I confess I don't understand why it is introduced, unless it be to cover a scene-change, and I can find no mention of bells or Sunday in the text ; but I am quite sure there is some good reason for this number, apart from its own beauty. It is *pianissimo*, scored for very high tremolo violins, celesta bells, and harp ; and I should very much like to know exactly what it means in its present position in the play.

Now comes a long and elaborate march of shepherds and shepherdesses, beginning in march time, four in a bar ; then the time changes to two in a bar, and a very wild dance follows. Again the time changes, to mazurka rhythm now, three in a bar, and a very graceful dance in this time follows ; finally we return to the fast two-in-a-bar passage, and the whole dance finishes with a coda, during which the music gets faster and faster to the end. The whole number makes a short ballet, with plenty of rhythmic changes. It is most effective, as well as being part of Shakespeare's plot.

Almost immediately comes Autolycus's song, " Lawn as white as driven snow " ; this also is very carefully set. The next number is very interesting. It is a trio, sung by Autolycus, Dorcas, and Mopsa, accompanied by a *bouche fermée* male-voice chorus—not singing the usual slow, sustained harmonies, but a quick four-part syncopated rhythm. This is a very ingenious number. After a little dialogue comes Autolycus's last song, " Will you buy any tape ? " to a simple tune with an elaborate accompaniment. The Satyrs' dance that follows is a good example of strong but grotesque dance music in its first theme, but the trio is sensuous and suave, and the number finishes with a repetition of the first theme and a short but brilliant coda on the same melody.

In the last scene of the fifth act we have music

again.   Paulina says, " Music, awake not ; strike ! " and
very mysterious music is played until Hermione moves ;
then occurs a fine theme for brass and strings, while
Hermione descends from the pedestal ; after which, with
a few pauses, the music continues to the end, when the
curtain falls very slowly on Shakespeare's own last words.
The melodrama music here is so superlatively good that
one hardly notices it, such is its absolute rightness.   The
situation, dramatically, is so strong that, though the music
also is very individual, it does not for a moment counteract
the strength of effect of the closing scene, but just helps it
to a complete finish.   Rarely has Shakespeare been better
served by his acolytes.

SHAKESPEARE'S SONGS

William Linley, born 1771, edited two volumes octavo of settings to Shakespeare's lyrics, called *Dramatic Songs*. Some of them are by Purcell, Arne, etc.; but unfortunately the majority are by the editor, who seems to have had no exaggerated respect for Shakespeare's text, but a very high opinion of his own powers.

Mr Linley has some very naïve remarks to make in the observations printed after the preface. Writing of the lyrics sung by Feste in *Twelfth Night*, he says: "Though there is a whimsical point about them, they are not inelegantly written." (This of "Come away, Death"!) Linley proceeds: "Shakespeare evidently meant that it should be sung with pathetic expression, but one is not prepared to relish it from the Clown; and there is nothing ludicrous in the words, and the plaintive wildness which they seem to demand from the music could not, by any aid of preparation, be given by the Clown so as to produce a feeling of melancholy—it would be more likely to excite laughter."

After these preliminary remarks, one may expect anything from our editor; and when one remembers the exquisite pathos of Mr Courtice Pounds' singing of **Augustus Barratt's** setting at His Majesty's one can smile at the pretentious want of knowledge displayed in Linley's short introduction.

His own setting, which is before me, is sorry stuff. Words and phrases are repeated over and over again. He does not even set the first sentence correctly; he says, "Come away, Death, come away," and continues his "improvement" throughout the song.

The same kind of thing occurs throughout his two volumes; but it is interesting to note that for a long time it was considered a standard work, and Roffe, so late as 1867, speaks of it in his *Handbook of Shakespeare Music* as " a happily conceived work."

It is a curious thing that the lyrics in the plays most popular with composers are either frankly not by Shakespeare or are very doubtful. The one most frequently chosen, " Take, oh take those lips away," from *Measure for Measure*, has been set, according to Roffe (1867), seventeen times ; and, according to a work not quite truthfully describing itself as *A List of All the Songs and Passages in Shakespeare which have been Set to Music*, thirty times. Now, the second verse, " Hide, oh hide," is un-doubtedly by Fletcher, from *The Bloody Brother*, and it is likely that Shakespeare merely quoted the first verse without acknowledgment, as he often did.

The next in order is " Orpheus with his lute." Roffe gives it sixteen settings, and *A List of all the Songs, etc.*, twenty-two ; the latter boldly states, " By John Fletcher." Act iii., Scene 1 is part of the Fletcher portion of *Henry VIII*. "Shakespeare wrote only 1168½ of the 2822 lines of the play ; the rest are Fletcher's." The editors responsible for this note are F. J. Furnivall and W. G. Stone.

" Come live with me " (*Merry Wives*) has been set, accord-ing to Roffe, sixteen times, and according to the " List " eighteen—the words being quoted from Kit Marlowe. " The Willow " song from *Othello* (Roffe six and the " List " eleven) is much older than Shakespeare, and is quoted by him from a long poem now in Percy's *Reliques*.

Very naturally, since these dates (1867 and 1884) many other settings of songs from Shakespeare's plays have been made. Still, these four, two certainly not Shakespeare's and two quite doubtful Shakespeares, keep ahead in the list of music composed for or concerning the plays. I have referred to the " List," and think it only fair to give an account of it. It was published for " The New Shakespeare Society," and compiled by J. Greenhill, the Rev. W. A.

Harrison, and F. J. Furnivall; but unfortunately it was published in 1884, and has not been brought up to date. Here one may find that composers were not content with juggling and altering Shakespeare's perfect lyrics, but chose chunks of blank verse and snippets of sonnets to set, for no earthly purpose that I can see. Some of the composers' selections are quite incomprehensible. Why **R. J. Stevens** should have chosen Prospero's magnificent lines, beginning " The cloud-capt towers, the gorgeous palaces," and made them into a glee for S.A.T.T.B.B., passes my wit to understand.

Also, why **Sir Henry Bishop** chose Sonnet 109, " Oh, never say that I was false of heart " (lines 1–4 and 13–14), or Sonnet 29, " When in disgrace with fortune " (lines 1–4 and 9–12), with several verbal alterations. All this tends to show that the composer could not have had the smallest conception of the sonnet form, to cut and chop it about as he has done. Personally, I think that no sonnet ought to be set to music, but I know that quite good musical authorities differ from me, and I am content to say that either the whole sonnet or none of it must be set. It is impossible to cut a word or a sentence out of a sonnet without spoiling its form and balance; and, if these essentials are gone, how can it make a perfect song ?

INDEX

PRINTED IN GREAT BRITAIN BY NEILL AND CO., LTD., EDINBURGH.